Chambers

SPORTING
QUOTATIONS

Simon James

Published 1990 by W & R Chambers Ltd,
43–45 Annandale Street, Edinburgh EH7 4AZ

British Library Cataloguing in Publication Data

Chambers sporting quotations.
1. Sports
I. James, Simon
796

ISBN 0–550–20489–X

Cover design by Keith Kail

Typeset by Pillans and Wilson Ltd, Edinburgh
Printed in England by Clays Ltd, St Ives plc

CONTENTS

INTRODUCTION

The quotations that follow are arranged by topic (from Amateurs to Wrestling) and a list of these appears on page vii. As some quotations do not fit neatly into only one topic, and because a whole range of other subjects are also touched upon, an Index of Key Words has been provided.

This index, which starts on page 221, gives a two-figure reference for each quotation in which the key word plays an important part. The first figure refers to the number of the topic and the second to the quotation itself. Part of the quotation is also given to indicate the context. For example, an entry under 'prize fightin'' reads 'hardest thing about p. 12.55'. This refers to the 55th quotation appearing under the 12th topic, which is Boxing, and the full quotation is 'I'll bet th' hardest thing about prize fightin' is pickin' up yer teeth with a boxin' glove on.' The numbers and titles of the topics appear at the top of the pages, and within each topic the quotations are arranged alphabetically by author or source. The Index of Key Words does not include words which are the same as the topics under which they appear.

There is also an Index of Authors and Sources which is referenced in the same way. This index appears at the end of the book not because it is in any sense less important than the Index of Key Words, but to make it slightly easier to find. While the years of birth and death have been given wherever possible for deceased authors from earlier periods, this has not been done for those who flourished in more recent years and certainly no attempt has been made to provide the year of birth for living persons.

Finally, I should like to express my gratitude for the generous and expert assistance of the staff of a number of libraries.

University of Exeter

Simon James

LIST OF TOPICS

1 AMATEURS

1   The artistic temperament is a disease that afflicts amateurs.
G. K. Chesterton (1874–1936)
Heretics, 1908, Ch. 17

2   Between the amateur and the professional ... there is a difference not only in degree but in kind. The skilful man is, within the function of his skill, a different integration, a different nervous and muscular and psychological organization ... A tennis player or a watchmaker or an airplane pilot is an automatism but he is also criticism and wisdom.
Bernard De Voto (1897–1955)
Across the Wide Missouri, 1947

3   In love as in sport, the amateur status must be strictly maintained.
Robert Graves (1895–1985)
Occupation: Writer

4   The amateur has an inalienable right to play like a pillock.
Dick Greenwood (with reference to rugby union)
The Times, 4 November 1985

5   Let's be honest—a proper definition of an amateur today is one who accepts cash, not cheques.
Jack Kelly Jr.
John Samuel, *The Guardian Book of Sports Quotes*, 1985

6   The attainment of a sporting goal involves a much purer sensation when money is not present, because the drive to succeed has come entirely from within.
David Kirk
Observer, 19 March 1989

7   The amateur element, infusing a spirit necessarily different to that ... possessed by the most hard-working of professionals, should be encouraged, even to the extent of including amateurs who do not quite rise up to the high professional standard.
A. E. Knight
The Complete Cricketer, 1906

8   We have to cut out all this amateur crap. It's phoney. We have to be openly professional, money on the table where everybody can see it.

Carl Lewis
Independent, 23 July 1988

9   Professional sport has become entertainment. It is merely a circus. Real sport is still the kingdom of the amateur.

Jim Manning
Tony Pawson, *Runs and Catches*, 1980, Ch. 4

10   Amateurism is an ethos, not a tablet of stone. The spirit never changes, but the working regulations do.

Keith Rowlands
Observer, 19 March 1989

11   English genius is anti-professional; its affinities are with amateurs.

George Santayana (1863–1952)
Attributed

2   ARCHERY

1   A perfyte archer must firste learne to knowe the sure flyghte of his shaftes, that he may be boulde always to trust them.

Roger Ascham (1515–68)
Toxophilus, 1545

2   What of the bow?
       The bow was made in England:
  Of true wood, of yew wood,
       The wood of English bows;
           So men who are free
           Love the old yew-tree
  And the land where the yew-tree grows.

Sir Arthur Conan Doyle (1859–1930)
The Song of the Bow

3   A good archer is not known by his arrows, but his aim.
Thomas Fuller (1654–1734)
Gnomologia, 1732, No. 135

>4   An archer keen I was withal,
>   As ever did lean on greenwood tree:
>And could make the fleetest roebuck fall,
>   A good three hundred yards from me.
>Though changeful times, with hard severe,
>   Has made me now these joys forgo,
>Yet my heart bounds when e'er I hear
>   Yoicks, hark away! and tally ho!
>   Thomas Love Peacock (1785–1866)
>   *Hark Away*

5   [We] walked over the fields of Kingsland and back again, a walk I think I have not taken these twenty years but puts me in mind of my boy's time, when I boarded at Kingsland and used to shoot my bow and arrows in these fields.
Samuel Pepys (1633–1703)
Diary, 12 May 1667

>6   *Like an arrow shot*
>   *From a well experienc'd archer hits the mark*
>   *His eye doth level at.*
>   *William Shakespeare (1564–1616)*
>   *Pericles*, 1608–9, Act I, Sc. I

7   Draw, archers, draw your arrows to the head!
William Shakespeare (1564–1616)
Richard III, 1592–93, Act V, Sc. III

3 ATHLETES

1   Athletes are wonderful subjects for studying human psychology and physiology because you avoid the ethical problems of stressing people. Whatever you want to study, somebody in sport does it for fun.
Anonymous researcher
New Scientist, 18 March 1989

2 Th' athletic fool, to whom what Heaven denied
Of soul, is well compensated in limbs.

John Armstrong (1709–79)
The Art of Preserving Health, 1744, Bk. III

3 International athletes these days don't need a coach. They need a lawyer.

Steve Cram
Sunday Times, 30 August 1987

4 I didn't want to retire from athletics having never been a champion. I am not the nearly man any more.

Peter Elliot
Independent, 'Quotes of the Week', 10 February 1990

5 No athlete is crowned but in the sweat of his brow.

St Jerome (*c.* 342–420)
Letter, XIV

6 The prize, the prize secure!
The athlete nearly fell.

James Mason Neale (1818–66)
Safe Home, Safe Home

7 His limbs were cast in manly mould,
For hardy sports or contest bold.

Sir Walter Scott (1771–1832)
The Lady of the Lake, 1810, I, XXI

8 To me an athlete who fails is one who does not maximize the use of their potential, not necessarily one who loses a race.

Cliff Temple
The Times, 29 July 1978

9 The athlete today is *not* an athlete, he's the centre of a team – doctors, scientists, coaches and so on.

Emil Zatopek
Sunday Times, 17 July 1977

4 ATHLETICS

1   In the past a sexy woman was one who lay on a sofa like an odalisque, smoking a cigarette. Now she is an athletic woman.

Hardy Amies
Observer, 'Sayings of the Week', 8 January 1984

2   Shot putters must have the five Ss – strength, speed, stamina, suppleness and skill.

Geoff Capes
Independent, 18 February 1989

3   Nothing good in athletics is developed overnight.

Sebastian Coe
New York Times, 13 September 1988

4   For me championships are what athletics has always been about.

Sebastian Coe
Independent, 20 January 1990

5   Why should an athlete become a sort of surrogate parent in so many American homes?

Howard Cosell
The Times, 19 September 1985

6   From the time she stopped her wars, Greece took to trifles and her prosperity let her drift into folly: she was all aglow with passion for athletics and horses.

Horace(Quintus Horatius Flaccus 65–8 BC)
Epistles, II, ii, 93

7   Men – athletes especially – have to be like King Kong. When we lose, we can't cry and we can't pout.

Carl Lewis
Observer, 'Sayings of the Week', 29 July 1984

8   Even athletes, concerned as they are with man's basest part, nonetheless endure blows and pain so that they may tire their opponent and strike when advantage, and not anger, prompts.

Seneca (4 BC–AD 65)
De Ira, Bk. II, Ch. XIV

5 BADMINTON

1   Shuttlecock, shuttlecock, tell me true
How many years have I to go through?
One, two, three . . .
Anonymous

2   Badminton is an easygoing game, and does not require the muscular exertion demanded in bowling and is quite jolly withal.

Anonymous nineteenth-century newspaper correspondent
George Sullivan, *Guide to Badminton*, 1968

3   It has long puzzled me why nobody expects to play the piano or the violin without hours and hours of practice, yet is disappointed when he cannot execute strokes of a racket game that have taken a champion years to perfect.

Fred Brundle
Teach Yourself Badminton, 1959, Ch. X

4   Take one shuttlecock, one racket and a kindred spirit similarly armed and hit the shuttlecock back and forth to each other. If you can carry out this simple task, then you can play badminton.

Ken Crossley
Progressive Badminton, 1970, Pt. I

5   Battledore and shuttlecock's a wery good game, vhen you an't the shutttlecock and two lawyers the battledores, in which case it gets too excitin' to be pleasant.

Charles Dickens (1812–70)
The Pickwick Papers, 1837, Ch. XX

6   Because I am thirty it doesn't mean I'm finished.

Morten Frost
Independent, 15 October 1988

7   Of all the abilities that are necessary to make a champion badminton player, deception is the most important and the hardest to achieve.

Judy Devlin Hashman
Badminton: A Champion's Way, 1969 Ch. 11

8 Boys and girls pick up the racket differently, and they move around the court differently. A strong woman will play like a mannish woman, but not like a man.

Judy Devlin Hashman
Sunday Times, 4 April 1982

9 Badminton is all go. All run and stop and turn and smash and stretch and stoop. All sweat, all strain.

David Hunn
Observer, 8 March 1987

10 Perhaps the most fascinating feature of the game of badminton is its versatility.

Waldo K. Lyon
Introduction to George Sullivan, *Guide to Badminton*, 1968

11 Badminton is predominantly a perceptual skill requiring an ability to anticipate without being anticipated.

Peter Roper
Badminton: The Skills of the Game, 1985, Ch. 1

6 BALLOONING

1 Anybody with good sense and basic athletic ability can do it.

Jerry P. Owens
New York Times, 19 September 1988

7 BASEBALL

1 Most managers fire themselves. They make mistakes. A big one is celebrity. Some managers take their celebrity serious. The TV publicity goes to their coconuts.

Sparky Anderson
New York Times, 19 June 1978

2   I've never seen a manager win a pennant. Players win pennants.

Sparky Anderson
New York Times, 11 May 1986

3   There's two kinds of ballplayers – prospects and suspects. And suspects don't like prospects.

Anonymous

> 4   Base Ball
> The ball once struck off,
>   Away flies the boy
> To the next destined post,
>   And then home with joy.
>
> Anonymous
> *A Pretty Little Pocketbook*, 1744

5   'In court', says the card on the lawyer's door,
'Back in ten minutes', on many more;
'Gone to hospital', on the doctor's slate,
On another, 'Sit down and wait'.
'Gone to the bank', on the notary's sign;
'Arbitration', that young clerk of mine.
'Back soon', on the broker's book;
'Collecting rents', on my agent's hook.
They were all too busy, a matter quite new,
Very sorry was I, I had nothing to do.
Then I hied me hands to the baseball ground,
And every man on the grandstand found.

Anonymous
Official Baseball record of 1886

6   After spending four years as a college star he was a failure at pro baseball. In fact all he had to show for it was an education.

Anonymous

7   It was not very wonderful that Catherine, who had by nature nothing heroic about her, should prefer cricket, baseball, riding on horseback and running around the country at the age of fourteen, to books.

Jane Austen (1775–1817)
Northanger Abbey, 1818, Ch. I

8   Although modern baseball is primarily American, urban, and male, its roots are medieval, English, rural and female.
William J. Baker
Sports in the Western World, 1982, Ch. 4

9   Whoever wants to know the heart and mind of America had better learn baseball.
Jacques Barzun
God's Country and Mine, 1954

10   Eighteen men play a game of baseball and eighteen thousand watch them, and yet those who play are the only ones who have any official direction in the matter of rules and regulations. The eighteen thousand are allowed to run wild.
Robert Benchley (1889–1945)
Rudolf Flesch, *The Book of Unusual Quotations,* 1959

11   You can't think and hit at the same time.
Yogi Berra
Laurence J. Peter, *Peter's Quotations,* 1977

12   You got to bat against a guy to know how fast he is.
Yogi Berra
New York Times, 8 May 1986

13   Bill Dickey taught me that catchin' isn't sittin', it's always movin' forward.
Yogi Berra
New York Times, 3 July 1988

14   You don't pitch with your birth certificate. If you can gamble with a twenty-year-old with a fast ball, you can gamble with a thirty-nine-year-old with a knuckle ball.
Jim Bouton
New York Times, 21 May 1978

15   Hitting a baseball could well be the single most difficult skill in sport.
Jim Bowen
Scholastic Coach, March 1980

16   I think [baseball]'s all right; it keeps the parents off the streets.
Rocky Bridges
Sports Illustrated, 2 March 1964

17   When you are a baseball player and know you can't do what you used to do, you feel bad. If you keep coming round the clubhouse, it just makes you feel pitiful because you want to come back.

Enos Cabell
New York Times, 28 September 1980

18   You gotta be a man to play baseball for a living but you gotta have a lot of little boy in you.

Roy Campanella
Laurence J. Peter, *Peter's Quotations*, 1977

19   I was built up to be some kind of monster robot. All you had to do was oil my joints and I'd hit 390 and lead the league in every category . . . If I'd hit forty this year, someone will say I should've hit fifty. And if I hit fifty, they'll say it should've been sixty.

Jose Canseco
Sports Illustrated, 12 September 1988

20 ·   People see me run, and they think I look lackadaisical, yet my stride is deceptive. The smaller guys just look as if they're running faster, with their quick little steps.

Jose Canseco
Independent, 15 October 1988

21   Last year everybody blamed me for losing the world series. They came up to me and said: 'Jose, I lost money because of you, I lost my house because of you, I lost my wife because of you, I began to drink because of you.' I told them all: 'Kiss my ass.' I mean, what am I, some sort of machine?

Jose Canseco
Observer, 15 October 1989

22   What's baseball when compared to death? What's baseball when compared to starvation? It's a game. I can go 20 for 20 or zero for 100. It's still a game.

Jose Canseco
Sunday Times, 15 October 1989

23   Any time you can trade a pitcher for an everyday player, you do it, unless the pitcher will turn into a Hall of Famer.

Frank Cashen
New York Times, 22 June 1983

24   Nobody roots for Goliath.
Norman Chamberlain
New York Times, 1 March 1987

25   I thought baseball was a sport when I became a commissioner. I was mistaken. The semi-bandits own it.
Happy Chandler
Sports Illustrated, 19 November 1962

26   Being a baseball catcher means you are always close to the umpire, which means he can hear any comments that are made. But that didn't stop me.
Ian Chappell
Cricket in our Blood, 1976, Ch. 2

27   Baseball creates its own time, and the fact that a baseball game could theoretically last forever is a comfort to its fans.
Stephen Collins
New York Times, 24 July 1977

28   I still love to catch a ball more than anything. Catching a ball is a little like sex for me.
Dave Concepción
New York Times, 3 July 1988

29   Ever since my first visit to America in 1928, I have firmly believed that baseball, with its horizontal throwing and batting actions, is the best preparation if one thinks of other sports as good training for golf.
Henry Cotton
Donald Steel, *The Golfer's Bedside Book,* 1971

30   The purist in me knows that games are won by pitching and defense. But the executive in me knows something else. Offense is what puts bodies in the seats.
Harry Dalton
New York Times, 3 July 1988

31   You don't save a pitcher for tomorrow. Tomorrow it may rain.
Leo Durocher
Laurence J. Peter, *Peter's Quotations,* 1977

32   The schoolboys went on with their game of baseball without regard to the passenger, and the ball struck him smartly in the back. He was angry. Little cared the boys. If you had learned how to play when you was at school, they said, you would have known better than to be hit. If you did not learn then, you had better stop short where you are, and learn now. Hit him again Dick!

Ralph Waldo Emerson (1803–82)
Journal, 5 April 1842

33   I'm not old, I was just born before a lot of other people.

Darrell Evans
New York Times, 30 September 1987

34   Every day I play I hear about how much money I got. It's like my last name. My name is 2.85 instead of Gamble.

Oscar Gamble (having signed a $2.85 million contract)
New York Times, 19 June 1978

35   A baseball team doesn't run out of time, it runs out of outs.

Robert Gensemer
Tennis, 1969, Ch. 1

36   Talking to Yogi Berra about baseball is like talking to Homer about the Gods.

A. Bartlett Giamatti
New York Times, 5 April 1987

37   A great catch is like watching girls go by – the last one you see is always the prettiest.

Bod Gibson
Sports Illustrated, 1 June 1964

38   In a way an umpire is like a woman. He makes quick decisions, never reverses them and doesn't think you're safe when you're out.

Larry Goetz, baseball umpire
James Beasley Simpson, *Best Quotes of '54, '55, '56*, 1957

39   Baseball is like hillbilly music – it's got to be performed with an American accent.

Michael Green
Sunday Times, 6 August 1978

40   It's funny how smart a manager you become when you get good pitching.
Whitey Herzog
New York Times, 3 July 1977

41   You hear more stories that Yogi [Berra] never said than those he did say.
Ralph Houk
New York Times, 3 July 1977

42   After a boy gets in a three-base hit, it takes a long time for his mother to get him under control again.
E.W. Howe (1853–1937)
Country Town Sayings, 1911

43   The new definition of a heathen is a man who has never played baseball.
Frank McKinney Hubbard (1868–1930)
Epigrams, 1923

44   Knowin' all about baseball is just about as profitable as bein' a good whittler.
Frank McKinney Hubbard (1868–1930)
Clifton Fadiman, *The American Treasury: 1455–1955*, 1955

45   I take a national view of the American League and an American view of the National League.
Hubert Humphrey
Sports Illustrated, 11 September 1967

46   Patience, that's what an older pitcher has that a younger pitcher doesn't . . . The only trouble is, when you're old, other people sometimes tend to lose patience with you quicker.
Tommy John
New York Times, 28 September 1980

47   It's always tougher to win when everyone expects you to.
Dave Johnson
New York Times, 23 September 1988

48   When I first became a manager, I asked Chuck [Tanner] for advice. He told me, 'Always rent.'
Tony LaRussa
Sports Illustrated, 27 August 1984

49   We'll win if the Big Dodger in the sky wills it.

Tommy Lasorda
John Samuel, *The Guardian Book of Sports Quotes*, 1985

50   Managing is knowing who to keep and who to get rid of.

Joe McCarthy
New York Times, 30 July 1978

51   Most males who don't care about big-league baseball conceal their indifference as carefully as they would conceal a laughable physical deficiency.

Russell Maloney
Clifton Fadiman, *The American Treasury: 1455–1955*, 1955

52   Nobody gets a kick out of baseball anymore, because big salaries and the pension fund have made it a more serious business than running a bank.

Rabbitt Maranville
Sports Illustrated, 27 August 1962

53   The only real way you know you've been fired, is when you arrive at the ball park and find your name has been scratched from the parking list.

Billy Martin
New York Times, 24 July 1977

54   Managing in the dugout is easy, it's the clubhouse that's the problem.

Billy Martin
New York Times, 25 July 1977

55   Everybody wants to hit someplace else in the batting order. That's why I picked the batting order out of the hat that day – to show them that it didn't make any difference where you hit if you hit.

Billy Martin
Ibid.

56   I saw Joe DiMaggio last night . . . and he wasn't wearing his baseball suit. This struck me as rather foolish. Suppose a ball game broke out in the middle of the night? By the time he got into his suit the game would be over.

Groucho Marx
Attributed

57   Rowdyism by the players on the field, syndicalism among the club owners, poor umpiring, and talk of rival organizations . . . are the principal causes accountable for baseball's decline.

New York Times, 1900
Quoted in William J. Baker, *Sports in the Western World*, 1982, Ch. 10

58   You can't be too nice to players or it'll backfire on you. There's no substitute for good discipline.

Lou Piniella
New York Times, 10 July 1978

59   You've got to generate power. It's just like a spring. You've got to tighten it up and generate power. You can't just stand up there. You've got to coil yourself.

Jim Rice
New York Times, 26 June 1978

60   Close doesn't count in baseball. Close only counts in horseshoes and grenades.

Frank Robinson
New York Times, 17 July 1978

61   There are no prizes for winning the first half.

Steve Rogers
New York Times, 22 July 1979

62   All I can tell 'em is I pick a good one and sock it. I get back to the dugout and they ask me what it was I hit and I tell 'em I don't know except it looked good.

George Herman ('Babe') Ruth
Clifton Fadiman, *The American Treasury: 1455–1955*, 1955

63   Tunnel-vision is how I explain it . . . You know that everything is going right and you become isolated from all outside distraction . . . and there's only you, the hitter and the catcher.

Nolan Ryan
New York Times, 18 May 1986

64   The only way you can learn in this game [baseball] is by going out and doing it.

Joe Sambito
New York Times, 8 July 1979

65   It's like being president of the Flat Earth Society.

Don Smallwood, the President of the British Baseball Federation (on the lack of
enthusiasm for the sport in Britain)
Independent, 'Quotes of the Week', 29 July 1989

66   Being a manager is simple. All you have to do is keep the five
players who hate your guts away from the five who are undecided.

Casey Stengel
John Samuel, *The Guardian Book of Sports Quotes*, 1985

67   Baseball is made up of streaks: good, bad and indifferent.
Right now, ours is bad.

Joe Torre
New York Times, 26 June 1978

68   The election of leaders in this country [USA] is far more
important than a baseball game. Having said that, I'd rather watch
a baseball game.

Peter Ueberroth
Independent, 'Quotes of the Week', 8 October 1988

69   Baseball is an island of surety in a changing world.

Bill Veeck
Jonathon Green, *A Dictionary of Contemporary Quotations*, 1982

70   Though it [baseball] is a team game by definition, it is actually
a series of loosely connected individual efforts.

Bill Veeck
Scholastic Coach, December 1983

71   Baseball gives every American boy a chance to excel, not just
to be as good as someone else but to be better than someone else.
This is the nature of man and the name of the game.

Ted Williams
Sports Illustrated, 8 August 1986

72   For the parent of a Little Leaguer, a baseball game is simply a
nervous breakdown divided into innings.

Earl Wilson
Attributed

73   Ninety per cent of baseball is half mental.

Jim Wohlford
John Samuel, *The Guardian Book of Sports Quotes*, 1985

8 BASKETBALL

1   Top basketball players have to be complete athletes, who work together as a team with almost electronic precision.

Vic Ambler
Basketball: Scoring Skills and Strategies, 1976, p. 9

2   Anyone can play basketball. All you need is a ball, small space and some kind of hoop attached to a wall, tree or pole.

Vic Ambler
Basketball, 1984, Ch. 1

3   Basketball is a game of momentum.

Vic Ambler
Ibid., Ch. 2

4   The teams that win are the teams with players who know the fundamentals, and who know the meaning of team ball.

Rick Barry
New York Times, 6 January 1977

5   We'll be playing like there's no tomorrow, because as far as this club's concerned, it looks like there won't be any tomorrows.

Kevin Cadle of Glasgow Rangers
Independent, 15 April 1989

6   The trouble with referees is that they just don't care which side wins.

Tom Canterbury
John Samuel, *The Guardian Book of Sports Quotes*, 1985

7   I feel I wouldn't have been a great basketball player if I hadn't been brought up in Philadelphia.

Wilt Chamberlain
New York Times, 6 May 1979

8   Basketball is a simple game and the successful teams do the simple things very well.

Brian E. Coleman
Basketball: Techniques, Teaching and Training, 1975, Introduction

9   Be at ease when you play.

Bob Cousey
Vic Ambler, *Basketball: Scoring Skills and Strategies*, 1976

10 A basketball coach is at once a teacher, a leader, a psychologist, a public relations liaison agent, and a professional man.

Bob Cousey and Frank G. Power
Basketball, 1979, Pt. 1 'The Coach'

11 Practice without reference to playing the full game produces 'circus performers'.

Len Hoy and Cyril A. Carter
Tackle Basketball, 1980, Ch. 9

12 I didn't hire Scott as assistant coach because he's my son. I hired him because I'm married to his mother.

Frank Layden
Sunday Times, 5 July 1987

13 As many coaches have stated, there are no secrets in basketball.

Jack Lehane
Basketball Fundamentals, 1981, Preface

14 A while back, a good woman basketball player was cute. Now, it's all business.

Nancy Lieberman
New York Times, 11 June 1978

15 It's OK to be a great basketball player, but the trick is to be a great human being. That's what endears you to the public long after your last basket has fallen.

Nancy Lieberman
New York Times, 18 May 1986

16 The free throw shot is both easy – and difficult.

Peter Mintoft (ed.)
Basketball, 1978, Ch. 2

17 To a much greater degree than with most athletic contests the outcome of basketball games is predictable.

Robert Rice
The Business of Crime, 1956, Pt. V, Ch. III, 'Basketball Fixer'

18 If you play with rules and rigidity, it cuts down on creativity

Oscar Schmidt
New York Times, 18 September 1988

19   Any shot is a good shot.
Oscar Schmidt
New York Times, 21 September 1988

20   One of the misconceptions about basketball is its style of play. No matter what the purists contend, it's a one-on-one game within the team concept.
Gene Shue
New York Times, 29 July 1979

21   It's better to eat caviar with two players than hot dogs with five.
Marcel Souza
New York Times, 21 September 1988

22   In basketball you pick up a couple of great players and a good supporting cast and you're there.
Eddie Sutton
New York Times, 3 March 1980

23   It is an unfortunate truism that practically every movement in basketball except running is artificial and unnatural.
Jerry Tarkanian and William E. Warren
Winning Basketball Systems, 1981, Ch. 13, 'Individual Fundamentals'

24   To say that a good defensive centre is more important than a high-scoring forward is like saying that the intestinal tract is more vital than the circulatory system.
Telford Taylor
New York Times, 20 May 1979

25   One might be forgiven for imagining that there were as many different games of basketball as there were players and coaches.
Vaughan Thomas
Basketball, 1972, Introduction

26   Basketball is such an emotional game for me, there is such ecstasy when you do really great and such frustration and anger when you don't.
Bill Walton
New York Times, 29 March 1987

27   The more you give the ball up, the more you get it back.
Joe Whetton
Step by Step Basketball Skills, 1988, 'Passing'

28   Basketball is a game of habits.
John R. Wooden
Practical Modern Basketball, 1966, Ch. 1

29   Three things are vital to success in basketball–condition, fundamentals, and working together as a team.
John Wooden
They Call Me Coach, 1972, Ch. 18

9   BILLIARDS

See also 88 Snooker

1   Royal Subscription Rooms–Mr Congdon, the Proprietor of these magnificent rooms is now engaged in fitting up a most splendid Billiard Table, the bed of which is composed, in a most tasteful manner, of stone. The plan is altogether novel, but where tried has been highly approved of: they are, however, rare, as there are but three similarly constructed Billiard Tables in the country, and this alone in the West of England.
Exeter Flying Post, 16 July 1835

2   The billiard sharp whom any one catches,
    His doom's extremely hard–
        He's made to dwell–
        In a dungeon cell
    On a spot that's always barred.
And there he plays extravagant matches
    In fitless finger-stalls
        On a cloth untrue
        With a twisted cue
    And elliptical billiard balls.
W. S. Gilbert (1836–1911)
The Mikado, 1885, Act II

3 Nearly every unsuccessful man we ever met was a good billiard-player.
E. W. Howe (1853–1937)
Country Town Sayings, 1911

4 *The Game of Billiards – Scientifically Explained and Practically Set Forth in a Series of Novel and Extra-ordinary, but Equally Practical Strokes.*
Edwin Kentfield
Title of Book, 5th ed., 1850

5 A man who wants to play billiards must have no other ambition. Billiards is all.
E. V. Lucas (1868–1938)
Character and Comedy, 1907

6 Up all of us, and to billiards; my Lady Wright, Mr Carteret, myself and every body.
Samuel Pepys (1633–1703)
Diary, 11 July 1665

7 After dinner to billiards, where I won an angel [a gold coin bearing the image of an angel].
Samuel Pepys (1633–1703)
Ibid., 11 September 1665

8 Let it alone; let's to billiards.
William Shakespeare (1564–1616)
Anthony and Cleopatra, 1606–7, Act II, Sc. V

9 It was remarked to me . . . that to play billiards well was a sign of a misspent youth.
Herbert Spencer (1820–1903)
Duncan, *Life and Letters of Herbert Spencer*, 1908, Ch. 20

10 Half the time often lost in learning to play the beautiful but pernicious game of billiards would be sufficient to give a youth master of that art [drawing].
John Wilson (Christopher North) (1785–1854)
Noctes Ambrosianae, 12

10 BOBSLEIGH

1 [Bobsleighing] is a sport which you do because of the element of risk. That's what gets the adrenalin going. It's very close to orgasmic, difficult to describe, a sense of relief and achievement. Which is what makes the bobsled community fairly close.

Mo Hammond
Observer, 1 February 1987

2 It's the speed, the adrenalin, and, once you get to know the sport, it's the skill involved. Most people think you just sit in the sled with your arms crossed. They don't realize you steer and how important the crew members are. People think they are just ballast.

Nick Phipps
Observer, 1 February 1987

3 You need sprinters and jumpers, people with leg strength and speed, because you have to be in good shape. It's no good if you're puffing after running and pushing for fifty metres at the start. Just by moving your backside you can make the sled veer off into the wall. When four men leap into the bob they have to be as one. In this sport half a second is an ocean. That's why everything has got to be right.

Nick Phipps
Ibid.

4 Take the danger element away from the sport, and it's just like any other, with the aim of getting down faster than anybody else.

Mark Tout
Independent, 11 February 1989

11 BOWLS

1 I talk to my bowls because that's my natural style – and I am not going to change it!

Laufili Pativaine Ainuu
The Times, 3 February 1990

2   The rub of the green.
Anonymous

3   Cahill's courage ... courage one can expect from a man whose father captains an Adelaide bowls team.
BBC
Private Eye, No. 720, 21 July 1989

4   Wipe out earth's furrows of the Thine and Mine,
And leave one green, for men to play Bowls,
With winnings for them all.
Elizabeth Barrett Browning (1806–61)
Aurora Leigh, 1857, Bk. II

5   As long as I can keep trundling them down, I hope I can keep winning.
David Bryant
The Times, 11 August 1978

6   There's no release in bowls. You can't run off the pressure as in soccer, or get rid of it with a bouncer, as they do in cricket. In golf you've not got the strain of knowing your opponent can destroy what you've built up.
David Bryant
Daily Telegraph, 2 March 1989

7   There's plenty of time to win this game and to thrash the Spaniards too.
Sir Francis Drake (1540?–96) (on hearing the news of the arrival of the Spanish Armada off the Lizard)
Quoted in *The Dictionary of National Biography*

8   The jack ought to possess a kind of sacred nature and rules made to prevent its being recklessly displaced.
W. J. Emmett
Attributed, 1914

9   To cure the mind's wrong biass, spleen,
Some recommend the bowling green.
Matthew Green
The Spleen, 1737

10   At some time in the early history of man someone, somewhere, picked up a round boulder and trundled it along the ground.

Alfred H. Haynes
The Story of Bowls, no date, Ch. 1

11   I'd rather play the men than the women because you know what the men are going to do. When you play against a man you're not playing for yourself, you're playing for every woman in the UK.

Margaret Johnston
Independent, 15 October 1988

12   All you run you win.

James Kelly (Kelly says this phrase is 'taken from playing at bowls; apply'd to endeavours about a project that seems not feasible, where what you can make is a clear gain')
Scottish Proverbs, 1721, A, No. 258

13   A successful partnership usually consists of one good player and one moderate player who usually plays above himself in the other's company.

E. A. Lundy
Crown Bowls, 1961, Ch. 5

14   Bowls was not always the peaceable and relaxing pastime that on the surface it appeared. It is, and can be, played with ferocious intensity.

Eric Midwinter
W. G. Grace: His Life and Times, 1981, Ch. 12

15   Never sacrifice direction for speed.

Albert Newton
The Fundamentals of Lawn Bowls, 1960, Ch. 10

16   The Bowling-ally, where lords and ladies are now at bowles, in brave condition.

Samuel Pepys (1633–1703)
Diary, 26 July 1662

17   O thou, of bus'ness and directing soul!
      To this our head like byass to the bowl,
      Which, as more pond'rous, made its aim more true,
      Obliquely waddling to the mark in view.

Alexander Pope (1688–1744)
The Dunciad, 1726

18   Three things are thrown away on a bowling green, namely,
time, money and oaths.

Sir Walter Scott (1771–1832)
The Fortunes of Nigel, 1822, Ch. XII

19   *Cloten:*   Was there ever a man had such luck! when I kissed
               the jack, upon an up-cast to be hit away! I had a
               hundred pound on't: and then a whoreson jack-
               anapes   must   take   me   up   for   swearing...

      Lord: What got he by that? You have broke his pate with
               your bowl.

William Shakespeare (1564–1616)
Cymbeline, 1609–10, Act II, Sc. I

20   What I have lost to-day at bowls I'll win tonight of him.

William Shakespeare (1564–1616)
Ibid.

21   *Costard:*   She's too hard for you at pricks, sir; challenge her
               to bowl.

      Boget: I fear too much rubbing; good night, my good owl.

William Shakespeare (1564–1616)
Love's Labour Lost, 1594–95, Act IV, Sc. I

22   An honest man, look you, and soon dashed! He is a
marvellous good neighbour, insooth; and a very good bowler.

William Shakespeare (1564–1616)
Ibid., Act V, Sc. II

23   *Queen:*   What sport shall we devise here in this garden?
              To drive away this heavy thought of care?

      Lady: Madam, we'll play at bowls.

      Queen: 'Twill make me think.
              The world is full of rubs, and that my fortune
              Runs against the bias.

William Shakespeare (1564–1616)
Richard II, 1595–96, Act III, Sc. IV

24 Well, forward, forward! thus the bowl should run,
And not unluckily against the bias.

William Shakespeare (1564–1616)
The Taming of the Shrew, 1593–94, Act IV, Sc. V

25 We really are a wonderful people, we bowlers. We are such sociable human folk. Let a stranger show but a passing interest and what do we do? We invite him to come along and take an end. Fancy a cricket team asking the onlookers to put down an over or two or have a turn at the wicket!

Robert Stanley
Bowls News, 1927

26 Bowls . . . remains a sport where not only the woods move slowly.

Richard Streeton
The Times, 3 December 1977

12 BOXING

1 I was worried until I heard you were betting on Frazier.

Muhammad Ali (to Joe Louis)
Muhammad Ali with Richard Durham, *The Greatest: My Own Story*, 1976, Ch. 17
(See also Cassius Clay below)

2 The title is always in danger. Every man has a chance to win. This is a dangerous sport.

Muhammad Ali
Sunday Telegraph, 31 July 1966

3 The most important was the second Spinks fight. Winning the title for the third time. Ending my career as a winner. That was the most important.

Muhammad Ali
New York Times, 1 July 1979

4 Talking and bragging made me fight better. I had to back up what I said.

Muhammad Ali
Ibid.

5   You can be rich or poor but you don't know nothin' about either until you felt pain.
Muhammad Ali
John Samuel, *The Guardian Book of Sports Quotes*, 1985

6   Boxing is a lot of white men watching two black men beat each other up.
Muhammad Ali
Attributed

7   As heavyweights go, so goes boxing.
Anonymous

8   Boxing is a science: it's really all up to the biffins.
Anonymous

9   It's hard to turn a gentle man into a tiger, but once you do, he's like a runaway lion.
Ray Barnes
Sunday Times, 22 May 1983

10   It's quite an embarrassment to be on the canvas.
Riddick Bowe
New York Times, 30 September 1988

11   So far as I know, the brain has no way of distinguishing a blow from a professional from a blow from an amateur.
Lord Brain (1895–1966) (on a Bill to prohibit professional boxing)
House of Lords, 10 May 1962

12   Nothing is going to stop Tyson that doesn't have a motor attached.
David Brenner
New York Times, 27 June 1988

13   May the day never come when an Englishman shall feel ashamed of it [boxing], or blackguards bring it to a disgrace.
John Broughton (1705–89)
Quoted by Viscount Scarsdale, House of Lords, 10 May 1962

14   My mum says I used to fight my way out of the cot. But I can't remember. That was before my time.
Frank Bruno
Private Eye, No. 642, 25 July 1986

15   I ain't no great showman. I ain't going to get flash and talk the ass off a donkey.
Frank Bruno
Observer, 'Sayings of the Year', 28 December 1986

16   That's cricket, Harry, you get these sort of things in boxing.
Frank Bruno
Private Eye, No. 676, 13 November 1987

17   There is only one God but not necessarily only one heavyweight champion.
Frank Bruno
Independent, 'Quotes of the Week', 8 October 1988

18   All I think about is winning the bleedin' title.
Frank Bruno
Observer, 'Sayings of the Year', 31 December 1989

19   My girlfriend boos me when we make love because she knows it turns me on.
Hector Camacho
Independent, 11 November 1989

20   They said it would last two rounds – they were half wrong, it lasted four.
Harry Carpenter
Private Eye, No. 574, 16 December 1983

21   He looks up at him through blood-smeared lips.
Harry Carpenter
Private Eye, No. 592, 24 August 1984

22   It's all right for the British Medical Association to talk about banning boxing. They have a qualified living. I've no qualifications. No job. Boxing is the best thing I can do. It's all I really know.
Errol Christie
Observer, 'Quotes of the Year', 19 December 1982

23   Boxers when striking their opponent, groan as they deliver the blow, not because they are in pain or losing heart, but because the groan makes their body more tense and the blow comes with greater force.
Marcus Tullius Cicero (106–43 BC)
Disputations, II, xxiii

24 I am the greatest! I am the king! I am the prettiest!

Cassius Clay, later Muhammad Ali (*see above*)
Observer, 'Sayings of the Year', 1964

25 I'm hoping we can fight again, or at least have a re-match.

John Conteh
Private Eye, No. 463, 14 September 1979

26 I took up boxing because it was the only way I could see of escaping poverty.

John Conteh
Observer, 'Sayings of the Week', 8 March 1981

27 No fighter comes into the ring hoping to win–he goes in hoping to win.

Henry Cooper
Private Eye, No. 575, 30 September 1983

28 Anything I got, I got through the fights.

Jack Dempsey
James Beasley Simpson, *Best Quotes of '54 , '55, '56*, 1957

29 Boxing is a strange business and if everything comes together a fighter can suddenly find himself.

James Douglas (on defeating Mike Tyson).
Independent ,13 February 1990

30 A lot of boxing promoters couldn't match the cheeks on their own backside.

Mickey Duff
Jonathon Green, *A Dictionary of Contemporary Quotations*, 1982

31 I only hope people will come along in peace and enjoy a good fight.

Mickey Duff, BBC Radio 4
Private Eye, No. 703, 22 November 1988

32 I am a fighter. Everybody likes a fighter.

Roberto Duran
Sunday Times, 3 December 1989

33   I don't think I'll ever miss boxing. I like the girls and the nice clothes and the fast cars and the money. And every time I see my name in the paper or my head on the TV I feel proud of my achievements. But the pressure is enormous.
Jeff Fenech
Sydney Morning Herald, 'Sayings of the Week', 19 July 1986

34   Boxers, who thrive in a cruel, unnatural sporting world, fight each other harder with words and insults before a bout than they may do in the ring. It is good publicity.
Jack Fingleton
Batting from Memory, 1981, Ch. 19

35   The fact you fellows didn't tip me at all took a great burden off my shoulders. I have never been tipped, except once, to win an ABA title and I lost that. When no one tipped me I won the national title.
Chris Finnegan (after winning the middleweight boxing Olympic gold medal)
The Times, 28 October 1968

36   I guess in this game you need to be a film star.
Chris Finnegan
The Times, 27 September 1972

37   The bigger they are the harder they fall.
Robert Fitzsimmons, 25 July 1902
Clifton Fadiman, *The American Treasury: 1455–1955*, 1955

38   Boxing is sort of like jazz. The better it is the fewer people can understand it.
George Foreman
Jonathon Green, *A Dictionary of Contemporary Quotations*, 1982

39   The other day at an airport I sat watching birds fly. They weren't intimidated by the big jets taking off into the sky. Flying comes naturally to them as fighting comes naturally to a fighter. Only those who have been in the ring can begin to know what I am talking about.
George Foreman
Independent, 18 October 1989

40   [Muhammad Ali] was so quick he would click off the light and be in bed before the room got dark.
George Foreman
The Times, 18 October 1989

41   If I miss the guy with the left and the right, I belly-bump him.

George Foreman
Independent, 'Quotes of the Week', 20 January 1990

42   I want to keep fighting because it is the only thing that keeps me out of hamburger joints. If I don't fight, I'll eat this planet.

George Foreman
Observer, 'Sayings of the Week', 21 January 1990

43   Seems everyone I've fought had a secret punch but I never got to see it.

Bob Foster
The Times, 22 September 1972

44   If I were a dictator, I would abolish prize fighting in my country by decree. I would scrap all rings, burn all boxing gloves and never let a youth be taught to strike another with his fist. For prize fighting and boxing are stupid, senseless, unappetizing inefficient and one hundred per cent useless.

Paul Gallico
Edith Summerskill, *The Ignoble Art,* 1956, p. 86

45   I hate the sight of blood .When I see it on an opponent's face I think I can't go on hitting him. I glance at the referee to encourage him to do something about it. If he won't, I'll go to the body or I'll throw a little flurry of punches to make the referee stop it.

Herol Graham
Sunday Times, 15 October 1989

46   The noble science of boxing is all our own. Foreigners can scarcely understand how we can squeeze pleasure out of this pastime; the luxury of hard blows given or received; the joy of the ring; nor the perseverance of the combatants.

William Hazlitt (1778–1830)
Merry England

47   Boxing's a great soap opera but at the moment it's *Coronation Street* without balls and I want it to be *Dallas* with balls.

Barry Hearn
Independent, 'Quotes of the Week', 30 September 1989

48 I am so happy I thought I was gonna cry. But I kept things in, and I just waved. It wouldn't be right for a world heavyweight champion to be crying.

Larry Holmes (on being welcomed by the population of Easton, PA, USA)
New York Times, 26 June 1978

49 When you're unbeaten, people think you ain't fought nobody. But to be unbeaten, you have to win every fight. Ali, he won the title three times, but that means he lost it twice.

Larry Holmes
New York Times, 31 March 1980

50 I've got a little bit of Muhammad Ali, a little Joe Louis and the determination of Sonny Liston. And if you shaved my head, I'd look like Jack Johnson.

Larry Holmes
Sunday Times, 6 June 1982

51 All the judges, the referees and the promoters can kiss me where the sun don't shine.

Larry Holmes (on losing a title fight)
Sydney Morning Herald, 'Sayings of the Week', 26 April 1986

52 Boxing is rough play, but not too rough for a hearty young fellow. Anything is better than this white-blooded degeneration to which we all tend.

Oliver Wendell Holmes (1809–94)
The Autocrat of the Breakfast Table, 1858, Ch. VII

53 If my young friend . . . could only introduce the manly art of self-defence among the clergy, I am satisfied that we should have better sermons and an infinitely less quarrelsome church-militant. A bout with the gloves would let off the ill-nature and cure the indigestion, which, united have embroiled their subject in a bitter controversy.

Oliver Wendell Holmes (1809–94)
Ibid.

54 Such admirably-ordered contests as that which I once saw at an English fair, where everything was done decently and in order, and the fight began and ended with such grave propriety that a sporting parson need hardly have hesitated to open it with a devout petition, and, after it was over dismiss the ring with a benediction.

Oliver Wendell Holmes (1809–94)
The Professor at the Breakfast Table, 1860 Ch. III

55   I'll bet th' hardest thing about prize fightin' is pickin' up yer teeth with a boxin' glove on.
Frank McKinney Hubbard (1868–1930)
Clifton Fadiman, *The American Treasury: 1455–1955*, 1955

56   The constant use of those surest keepers of the peace, the boxing gloves, kept the School-house boys from fighting one another.
Thomas Hughes (1822–96)
Tom Brown's Schooldays, 1857, Pt. II, Ch. V

57   Learn to box then, as you learn to play cricket and football. Not one of you will be the worse, but very much the better for learning to box well. Should you never have to use it in earnest, there's no exercise in the world so good for the temper, and for the muscles in the back and legs.
Thomas Hughes (1822–96)
Ibid.

58   Joe Louis was to America, what David was to Israel.
Jesse Jackson
New York Times, 13 May 1979

59   With fighters getting faster and stronger, maybe they will now be able to kill with one punch.
Ingemar Johansson
Quoted by Lord Taylor, House of Lords, 26 November 1981

60   I call it my check-hook, I check to see if he's there, then I throw it.
Ray Jones
New York Times, 27 September 1988

61   People in boxing is against me. People is jealous and envious. I'm like a diamond in the mud.
Sugar Ray Leonard
Sunday Times, 20 September 1981

62   What helped me develop my quickness was fear. I think the rougher the opponent, the quicker I am.
Sugar Ray Leonard
John Samuel, *The Guardian Book of Sports Quotes*, 1985

63   The desire to fight is inexplicable. But it brings my life into sharper focus. Whatever else I can imagine for myself it remains what I do best.

Sugar Ray Leonard
Independent, 1 December 1988

64   My legs are my energy, my escape route.

Sugar Ray Leonard
Attributed

65   It was a very happy fight. I was enjoying hitting him and he enjoyed getting hit.

Lennox Lewis
Independent, 'Quotes of the Week', 30 September 1989

66   A boxing match is like a cowboy movie. There's got to be good guys and there's got to be bad guys. That's what the people pay for, to see the bad guys get beat.

Sonny Liston
Jonathon Green, *A Dictionary of Contemporary Quotations,* 1982

67   He can run but he can't hide.

Joe Louis (interview before the second Louis–Conn fight)
Clifton Fadiman, *The American Treasury: 1455–1955*

68   I knew how to beat Rocky [Marciano]. Just jab, jab, jab and cross a right. Rocky was insulted if you missed him.

Joe Louis
New York Times, 13 May 1979

69   Every time you get in the ring it's a fight. A real fight.

Barry McGuigan
Sunday Times, 3 June 1984

70   In his prime, Bugner had the physique of a Greek statue, but he had fewer moves.

Hugh McIlvanney
Sydney Morning Herald, 'Sayings of the Week', 9 August 1986

71   Boxing has been my world; it's been everything to me. I want to do everything I can to help boxing. I want to try to tell youngsters how good it can be.

Rocky Marciano
James Beasley Simpson, *Best Quotes of '54, '55, '56,* 1957

72   Once in the ring, it don't matter how many people are watching. They won't be able to help.
Terry Marsh
Sunday Telegraph, 1 March 1987

73   I never had any ambitions to be a boxing champion. In fact if I had the time again I wouldn't want to be one. I'd rather study to be a businessman because it's a much better life.
Gary Mason
The Times, 4 February 1989

74   I aim to prove that I'm the boxer some people say I am, and some people say I'm not.
Gary Mason, BBC Radio 2
Private Eye, No. 726, 13 September 1989

75   A boxer makes a comeback for one of two reasons: either he's broke or he needs the money.
Alan Minter
Private Eye, No. 689, 13 May 1988

76   Boxing has . . . immense value. It teaches you never – that it is a disaster – to lose your temper, that there can be great nobility in losing, that fear lies in the heart and mind and that skill will always beat might.
Lord Morris
House of Lords, 26 November 1981

77   Boxing is probably the best and most individual lifestyle you can have without being a criminal.
Randy Neumann
Jonathon Green, *A Dictionary of Contemporary Quotations*, 1982

78   Nothing can match the blatant crudities of the preamble to a big fight.
Michael Parkinson
Sporting Fever, 1974

79   Boxing helps me relax. There's nothing like hitting someone to work out your frustrations.
Patrick Passley
The Times, 27 January 1990

80   Actually I've never retired. I just stopped fighting in 1972.
Floyd Patterson
New York Times, 29 September 1980

81 For ageing boxers, first your legs go. Then your reflexes go, then your friends go.

Willie Pep
Jonathon Green, *A Dictionary of Contemporary Quotations*, 1982
(*See also* Lord Taylor *below*)

82 Boxing is an artificial sport, unlike running, jumping or swimming – it is of extremely little value against a man armed with a weapon or a judo expert or strong and scientific wrestler. Fair play is a moral that has to be taught, and boxing is designed to teach it.

Viscount Scarsdale
House of Lords, 10 May 1962

83 The glove which I have given him for a favour
May haply purchase him a box o' the ear.

William Shakespeare (1564–1616)
Henry V, 1598–99, Act IV, Sc. VII

84 Give him a box o' the ear, and that will make 'em red again.

William Shakespeare (1564–1616)
Henry VI Pt. II, 1590–91, Act IV, Sc. VII

85 I see two chaps in the ring; I hit the one that isn't there, and the one that is there hits me.

Billy Softly (on the difficulty of double vision)
Quoted by Baroness Summerskill, House of Lords, 10 May 1962

86 Don't holler at me momma, I just lost the fight, that's all.

Leon Spinks
New York Times, 25 June 1979

87 A draw don't hurt nobody. Nobody wins, nobody loses and everybody comes back to fight again.

Leon Spinks
New York Times, 9 March 1980

88 Boxing is the best job in the world to let off steam, and people are in trouble when Tyson wants to let off steam.

Michael Spinks
Sydney Morning Herald, 'Sayings of the Week', 25 February 1989

89 My policy is don't fight the fighters and don't box the boxers.

Marlon Starling
Observer, 29 January 1989

90   The nation's morals, which had slowly crumbled, were being overthrown by imported licentiousness . . . that our youth, under the influence of foreign tastes, should degenerate into devotees of the gymnasium, of indolence and of unnatural vice . . .   What remained but to strip to the skin as well, put on boxing gloves, and practise that form of conflict instead of the profession of arms.
Tacitus (AD c. 55–c. 120)
Annals, XIV, xx

91   Among the boxing fraternity there is an adage: first the timing goes; then the legs; then the money; and then the friends. That is certainly the history of many of the people who have sought, through boxing, to achieve an easy way to riches.
Lord Taylor of Gryfe, House of Lords, 26 November 1981
(*See also* Willie Pep *above*)

92   Bugner was so ugly I couldn't consider making him uglier.
James Tillis
Guardian, 21 March 1987

93   OK, I'm the youngest-ever heavyweight champion: my only ambition now is to be the oldest.
Mike Tyson
Guardian, 21 March 1987

94   My objective is to be the ultimate professional. Regardless of whatever happens, the job has to be done. That's what being a professional is.
Mike Tyson
New York Times, 28 June 1988

95   Sometimes it's not easy being Mike Tyson.
Mike Tyson
The Times, 31 August 1988

96   Listen, if I chopped off one of my arms, he [Bruno] still couldn't beat me.
Mike Tyson
Independent, 'Quotes of the Week', 22 October 1988

97   [Boxing] . . . the hurt business.
Mike Tyson
Daily Telegraph, 25 February 1989

98   Sometimes I hit a guy with a punch I thought had missed. I say to myself 'Did I hit him?' – and he's lying there snoring.

Mike Tyson
Independent, 'Quotes of the Week', 25 February 1989

99   Once you get hit that helps me more than anything 'cos you calm down and say to yourself 'let's fight'.

Mike Tyson
Independent, 10 February 1990

100   I'm no longer a sportsman. How can you call professional boxing a sport, with all the villains and rogues who are part and parcel of the game? It's a business. A hard business all the time, a cruel business some of the time. I've no illusions about the noble art of self-defence or any of that kid stuff. That's all right for the amateurs but from now on I'm paid to hurt. The more I hurt the more I get paid.

Billy Walker (on turning professional in 1962)
Quoted by Baroness Summerskill, House of Lords, 10 May 1962

101   One would think that in an age of unemployed doctors, the British Medical Association might support the noble art of boxing on the grounds that it provides more work for them. Instead . . . [they] . . . have voted to ban the sport altogether.

Auberon Waugh
Private Eye, No. 589, 13 July 1984, 'Auberon Waugh's Diary'

13   CANOEING

1   That's canoeing. Like banging your head against a brick wall, it's gorgeous when you stop.

Sylvia Jackson
The Times, 24 October 1968

2   I think it much better that . . . every man paddle his own canoe.

Frederick Marryat (1792–1848)
Settlers in Canada, 1840, Ch. 8

3   But now the salmon-fishers moist
     Their leathern boats begin to hoist;
     And, like Antipodes in shoes,
     Have shod their heads in their canoes.
     How tortoise-like, but not so slow,
     These rational amphibii go!

Andrew Marvell (1621–78)
Upon Appleton House, to my Lord Fairfax

14 CARRIAGE-DRIVING

1   There is something endearingly domestic, hard-working and amateur about the world of competitive carriage-driving.

Libby Purves
Sunday Telegraph, 1 September 1985

15 CAVING

1   Caving is the most absolute of sports. It matches the thrills of exploring the unknown and defying physical obstacles with the intellectual challenge to explain how the unfamiliar shapes and beauties of underground scenery have evolved.

C.D.H. (Cecil) Cullingford
British Caving, 1953, Introduction

2   Caving is a physical adventure which leads to adventures of the mind.

Cecil Cullingford
Caving, 1976, 'Caving'

3   Caving is like good poetry, for it draws on all the senses as much as the emotions.

David Heap
Potholing Beneath the Northern Pennines, 1964, Ch. 1

4   It is a matter of historical fact that after each of the cave-diving deaths in the British Isles, active cave-diving has virtually ceased for a number of years and progress has been severely retarded.

Dr Ken Pearce
James Lovelock, *Caving,* 1969, Ch. 7

5   Britain's cave story is half human achievement, half nature's.

Donald Robinson and Anthony Greenbank
Caving and Potholing, 1964, Ch. 1

16 CHARIOT RACING

See also 45 Harness Racing

1   I am not a great fan of racing, but if you like one of the drivers then I'll support him too. I'm only here to be with you and tell you how I feel about you. You look at the races and I'll look at you. Then we shall both be looking at what we like. What a lucky man your favourite charioteer is, whoever he may be. I wish it were me.

Ovid (43 BC – AD 17)
Amores, III, 2

2   The Races were on, a type of entertainment which has never had the slightest attraction for me. I can find nothing new or different in them, and once you have seen one you have seen them all. It astonishes me that so many thousands of grown men should have such a childish passion for watching galloping horses and men standing in their chariots, over and over again. One could understand it if they were attracted by the speed of the horses or the skill of the drivers, but all they really care about are the racing colours. If the colours were to be exchanged during a race, the supporters would also transfer their favour and enthusiasm.

Pliny the Younger (Gaius Plinius Caecilius Secundus, AD c. 61–c. 112)
Letters, IX, vi

17 COACHING

1   Coaching an athlete is about marrying up commitment and imagination with a sense of reality. And I've always thought it was my business to take an athlete to the absolute limits of what they are capable.

John Anderson
Sunday Telegraph, 4 February 1990

2   Am I the most expensive coach in the world? If I win titles I am cheap.

Johan Cruyff
Independent, 'Quotes of the Week', 14 January 1989

3   One reason I'm a good coach is I'm always coaching scared. What frightens me most is having an athlete worse off being coached by me.

Bob Kersee
Independent, 'Quotes of the Week', 30 July 1988

4   Coaching so often has little to do with your ability or competence but only whether that scoreboard ends in your favour.

Sam Wyche
New York Times, 26 September 1988

18 CONKERS

1   Conkers is bonkers.

Anonymous

2   Women are to be excluded from the eleventh annual conker championships at Oundle. Our event would be ridiculed if women competed.

Frank Elson
John Samuel, *The Guardian Book of Sports Quotes*, 1985

19 COURSING

See also 41 Greyhound Racing

1   It is sacrilege to kill the hare. [Hare-coursing] is, in fact, the oldest and gentlest of the country sports.

Peter Howe
Independent, 20 October 1989

2   Edward and Richard, like a brace of greyhounds
Having the fearful flying hare in sight,
With fiery eyes sparkling for very wrath.

William Shakespeare (1564–1616)
Henry VI Pt. III, 1590–91, Act II, Sc. V

3   Say thou wilt course; thy greyhounds are as swift
As breathed stags; ay, fleeter than the roe.

William Shakespeare (1564–1616)
The Taming of the Shrew, 1593–94, Induction, Sc. II

4   O, sir, Lucentio slipp'd me like his greyhound,
Which runs himself, and catches for his master.

William Shakespeare (1564–1616)
Ibid., Act V, Sc. II

5   By an irony, this, one of the most execrated of field sports [hare- coursing], is the only one where killing the prey is positively not desired.

Geoffrey Wheatcroft
Sunday Telegraph, 1 March 1987

20 CRICKET

1   No runs from that over bowled by Jack Young, which means that he now has four maidens on the trot!

Rex Alston
Brian Johnston, *Rain Stops Play*, 1979, 'Slips'

2 This game [cricket] is unique, its roots were old when the Tudors were young, it combines combat with chivalry, it demands the most complete subordination of the individual to the interests of his team, and at the same time offers him the widest chance of self-expression.

H.S. Altham (1888–1965)
H. Doggart, *The Heart of Cricket*, 1967, p. 23

3 If you are going to cut, cut hard.

Anonymous
Trevor Bailey, *Sir Gary*, 1976, Ch. 8

4 It is still true that an umpire is the only single person who, alone, can make or ruin a game of cricket.

John Arlott
Foreword to Tom Smith, *Cricket Umpiring and Scoring*, 1980

5 Nothing is ever so disconcerting for a bowler as to have one ball driven 'over the top' and the next cut for four.

John Arlott
Jack Hobbs: Profile of 'The Master', 1981, Ch. 6

6 The really good wicketkeeper is completely unobtrusive, unless he makes a mistake. You ought not to notice him: in other words, his skill should have the air of inevitability.

John Arlott
How to Watch Cricket, 1983 ed., Ch. 8

7 Every now and then fast bowlers come out with the odd word that they should not come out with, which is perfectly reasonable. It is a man's game, after all.

Colin Atkinson
The Times, 30 December 1986

8 The big hitter in cricket who is also a genuine batsman is like the top-class golfer with a tremendous drive.

Trevor Bailey
Sir Gary, 1976, Ch. 8

9 If Viv Richards scores 80 there is no one in the Kent side capable of scoring an 80 of equal magnitude.

Trevor Bailey
Private Eye, No. 538, 30 July 1982

10   No captain with all the hindsight in the world, can predict how the wicket is going to play.
Trevor Bailey
Private Eye, No. 565, 12 August 1983

11   We owe some gratitude to Gatting and Lamb, who breathed some life into a corpse which had nearly expired.
Trevor Bailey
Private Eye, No. 602, 25 January 1985

12   It's funny how runs breed runs.
Ken Barrington
Playing It Straight, 1986, Ch. 11

13   It takes time to learn about captaincy, though to hear the experts talk you wouldn't think so.
Alec Bedser
The Times, 30 August 1980

14   They said to me at the Oval, come and see our new bowling machine. Bowling machine? I said. I used to be the bowling machine.
Alec Bedser
Sunday Telegraph, 5 March 1989

15   A lot of people will tell you there are more important things in the world than cricket.
Richie Benaud
Foreword in Trevor Bailey, *Sir Gary,* 1976

16   I do love cricket – it's so very English.
Sarah Bernhardt (1844–1923)
Attributed

17   If there were an Olympic event for running backwards, I would be the obvious favourite.
Dickie Bird
Not Out, 1978, Ch. 1

18   The Oval, the graveyard of bowlers.
Dickie Bird
Ibid., Ch. 10

19   We're all crackers to stand here for six and a half hours a day, but cricket's my life.
Dickie Bird
Sunday Telegraph, 'Quotes 1989', 24 December 1989

20   In the social set-up of modern India, cricket is the one sure way to gain acceptance.
Mihir Bose
Observer, 'Sayings of the Week', 10 January 1982

21   The day I worry about being hurt in cricket is the day I'll pack in the game.
Ian Botham
Dudley Doust, *Ian Botham: The Great All Rounder,* 1980, Ch. 1

22   You can't decide how you're going to play a ball before it's delivered.
Ian Botham
Observer, 'Sayings of the Week', 30 August 1981

23   It seems everything I do people are going out of their way to knock down.
Ian Botham
Observer, 'Sayings of the Week', 23 March 1986

24   If I'd done a quarter of the things of which I'm accused, I'd be pickled with alcohol. I'd be a registered drug addict and would have sired half the children in most of the world's cricket-playing countries.
Ian Botham
Sydney Morning Herald, 'Sayings of the Week', 12 April 1986

25   How am I going to live without cricket?
Ian Botham
Observer, 'Sayings of the Week', 1 June 1986

26   I have been to many functions where some great cricketers of the past have been present. To see some of them sink their drink is to witness performances as awe-inspiring as ever any of them displayed on the cricket field.
Ian Botham
The Times, 1 January 1987

27   They [newspaper reporters] are not here for the cricket. It's more a matter of Botham hasn't done anything; there must be something going on; let's stitch him up.
Ian Botham
Sydney Morning Herald, 'Sayings of the Week', 7 February 1987

28   You're never too old to stop learning.
Ian Botham
Private Eye, No. 711, 17 March 1989

29   You are only as good as your last game.
Ian Botham
BBC Radio 4, 15 August 1989

30   I'll decide when I write my obituary.
Ian Botham, BBC Radio 4
Private Eye, No. 726, 13 September 1989

31   The game itself might be compared to other more generous liquors: exhilarating and exciting is it, like champagne; beneficial, cordial, and fortifying to the system even as port; or it may be better likened for its infinite variety to that nectarious compound of all that is exquisite in beverage – the old-fashioned punch.
Charles Box
The English Game of Cricket, 1877

32   I did not put a rose down my flies. I did not call Raman Subba Row a wog. I did not ask for Ken Barrington's first-class ticket when he died.
Geoff Boycott
Observer, 'Sayings of the Week', 28 February 1982

33   Test matches are won by long innings, not brief, hard-hitting ones, however spectacular they may seem.
Geoff Boycott
John Callaghan, *Boycott: A Cricketing Legend,* 1982, Ch. 2

34   There is more to being a captain then just looking at one situation and deciding what to do.
Geoff Boycott
Ibid., Ch. 6

35   I always recommend to batsmen in Test matches: look at the scoreboard and add two wickets to the score; that's a cautionary view of what your position really is. It's a strange fact, but if you lose one wicket in Test cricket another usually follows very quickly.

Geoff Boycott
In the Fast Lane, 1982, Ch. 7

36   Cowans should remember what happened to Graham Dilley, who started out as a genuinely quick bowler. They started stuffing 'line and length' into his ear, and now he has Dennis Lillee's action with Denis Thatcher's pace.

Geoff Boycott
Observer, 'Quotes of the Year', 19 December 1982

37   People have a herding instinct. If a guy does not drink and goes off to practice or have dinner they think you are weird. You are not. You are different.

Geoff Boycott
Observer, 'Sayings of the Week', 7 June 1987

38   If you can't always play like a cricketer you can at least look like one.

Sir Donald Bradman
Ray Illingworth, *Yorkshire and Back,* 1980, Ch. 18

39   Cricket is a second-guessers' game. Worse even than baseball.

Mike Brearley
Sunday Times, 14 August 1977

40   Alderman knows that he is either going to get a wicket – or he isn't.

Steve Brenkley
Private Eye, No. 588, 29 June 1984

41   When we were children we asked my Uncle Charles what it was like to play cricket with W.G. Grace. 'The dirtiest neck I ever kept wicket behind,' was his crisp reply.

Lord Chandos
Observer, 'Sayings of the Week', 21 June 1959

42   It behoves all cricketers to remember that they must provide entertainment and be aware of cricket's overall well-being.
Greg Chappell
The Times, 15 August 1980

43   The greatest disaster in my life was when I lost the captaincy of England.
Brian Close
Doug Ibbotson, *Sporting Scenes*, 1980, Ch. 4

44   [There is] the need to teach people how to think. That is what is missing in English cricket.
Brian Close
Guardian, 12 October 1989

45   I think some of England's batsmen hold the bat so loosely now that West Indies fast bowlers actually twist the bat in their hands if the ball does not strike the middle of the blade.
Henry Cotton
The Times, 7 July 1984

46   At times you can run up and bowl an orange and it will do something.
Chris Cowdrey
Independent, 'Quotes of the Week', 30 July 1988

47   If I could turn the clock back twenty years I'd have picked a career in golf instead.
Ted Dexter
Independent, 'Quotes of the Week', 18 February 1989

48   The selectors' role should be to select and no more.
Ted Dexter
Guardian, 9 March 1989

49   What people want now is a group of likeable and watchable cricketers who play confidently with excellent results. You can't do anything about it if the opposition is better than you.
Ted Dexter
Sunday Times, 12 March 1989

50   People make comparisons with golfers. But golfers' whole business is keeping calm. Cricket is a hot-blooded game. We mustn't be too critical if young men, stretched to the limit, boil over. They may have to be simmered down pretty quickly but we shouldn't be too hard on them.
Ted Dexter
Guardian, 31 March 1989

51   If she [Mrs Thatcher] had been running cricket, England would be better off than they are.
Ted Dexter
Independent, 'Quotes of the Week', 6 May 1989

52   What young men and young ladies get up to in the evenings during a Test Match doesn't worry me a bit.
Ted Dexter
Observer, 'Sayings of the Year', 31 December 1989

53   You should play every game as if it's your last, but make sure you perform well enough to ensure it's not.
John Embury
Independent, 'Quotes of the Week', 9 July 1988

54   There's no more amateurish professional game in the world [cricket].
John Embury
Independent, 23 March 1989

55   Being a cricketer is worse than being a pop star for the family man – a pop star will take his wife along.
Mike Gatting
Independent, 'Quotes of the Week', 9 September 1989

56   Cricket is certainly a very good and wholesome exercise, yet it may be abused if either great or little people make it their business.
Gentleman's Magazine, 1743

57   Going out there and batting well takes steel.
David Gower
Observer, 'Sayings of the Week', 9 April 1989

58   I don't want to have to keep on saying, 'I want to win, I want to win, I want to win.' That is actually part of my make-up.
David Gower
Independent, 'Quotes of the Week', 15 April 1989

59   Test cricket involves using any weapon you've got, to its limit.

David Gower
Independent, 29 July 1989

60   It's hard work making batting look effortless.

David Gower
Sunday Telegraph, 'Quotes 1989', 24 December 1989

61   They came to see me bat not to see you bowl.

W.G. Grace (1848–1915) (on refusing to leave the crease having been bowled out by the first ball)
Attributed

62   Yes, he's a very good cricketer – pity he's not a better batter or bowler.

Tom Graveney
Private Eye, No. 671, 4 September 1987

63   The very names of a cricket bat and ball make English fingers tingle. What happy days must 'Long Robinson' have passed in getting ready his wickets and mending his bats, who, when two of the fingers on his right-hand were struck off by the violence of a ball, had a screw fastened to it to hold the bat, and with the other hand still sent the ball thundering against the boards that bounded *Old Lord's cricket-ground!*

William Hazlitt (1778–1830)
Merry England

64   Cricket is full of glorious chances, and the goddess who presides over it loves to bring down the most skilful player.

Thomas Hughes (1822–96)
Tom Brown's Schooldays, 1857, Pt. II, Ch. VIII

65   The discipline and reliance on one another which it [cricket] teaches is so valuable . . . it ought to be such an unselfish game. It merges the individual in the eleven; he doesn't play that he may win, but that his side may.

Thomas Hughes (1822–96)
Ibid.

66   You don't play this game for fun, Robin.

Sir Leonard Hutton
Attributed

67   Brain for the game . . . I played with plenty of good players but not all of them were good thinkers.

Sir Leonard Hutton
Observer, 2 July 1989

68   You do not always get as good a picture on the field as you do off it because the captain's job is so engaging.

Sir Leonard Hutton
Ibid.

69   There is no shortage of advice offered when things are not going so well.

Sir Leonard Hutton
Ibid.

70   One of the first things I look for in any young cricketer is: is he thinking? That is why so many reach a certain stage and go no further.

Sir Leonard Hutton
Ibid.

71   That's what batting's all about – knowing where the stumps are.

Ray Illingworth, BBC 1
Private Eye, No. 721, 4 August 1989

72   The bowler's Holding, the batsman's Willey.

Brian Johnstone
Stephen Winkworth, *Famous Sporting Fiascos,* 1982, Ch. 11

73   If the wild bowler thinks he bowls,
    Or the batsman think's he bowled,
  They know not, poor misguided souls,
    They too shall perish unconsoled.
  I am the batsman and the bat,
    I am the bowler and the ball,
  The umpire, the pavilion cat,
    The roller, pitch, and stumps, and all.

Andrew Lang (1844–1912)
Brahma

74   There is no talk, none so witty and brilliant, that is so good as cricket talk, when memory sharpens memory, and the dead live again – and the old happy days of burned-out June revive. We shall not see them again. We lament that lost lightness of heart, 'for no man under the sun lives twice, outliving his day', and the day of the cricketer is brief.

Andrew Lang (1844–1912)
Richard Daft, *Kings of Cricket*, 1893, Introduction

75   And where is Lambert, that would get
         The stumps with balls that broke astray?
      And Mann whose balls would ricochet
         In almost an unholy way,
      (So do baseballers 'pitch' today):
         George Lear, that seldom let a bye,
      And Richard Nyren, grave and grey?
         Beneath the daisies, there they lie!

      Andrew Lang (1844–1912)
      Ballade of Dead Cricketers

76   When I hear the commentators today saying: 'Oh, what a beautiful bouncer, it only just missed his head,' I wonder what the game has come to. I might sometimes have bowled at a batsman's ribs, but never at his head.

Harold Larwood
The Times, 3 February 1990

77   Men just don't like women umpires. They really do prefer to be given out by a man. When a woman gives them out, they fume, they walk up and down, they get very cross indeed.

Teresa McLean
The Times, 1 July 1987

78   If more girls' schools taught the game, women's cricket would be less of a joke.

Teresa McLean
Ibid.

79   Cricket is not a game. It's a way of life.

Michael Melford
Observer, 8 February 1987

80 There's a breathless hush in the Close tonight –
  Ten to make and the match to win –
A bumping pitch and a blinding light,
  An hour to play and the last man in.
And it's not for the sale of a ribboned coat,
  Or the selfish hope of a season's fame,
But his Captain's hand on his shoulder smote –
  'Play up! play up! and play the game!'

Sir Henry Newbolt (1862–1938)
Vitaï Lampada

81 I am not my brother's wicketkeeper.

Clyde Packer
Melbourne *Age*, 31 December 1977
Bill Wannan, *Great Aussie Quotes*, 1982

82 Everyone knows which comes first when it's a question of cricket or sex – all discerning people recognize that.

Harold Pinter
Observer, 'Sayings of the Week', 12 October 1980

83 Jackson's pace is very fearful, Willsher's hand is very high;
William Caffyn has good judgment, and an admirable eye;
Jemmy Grundy's cool and clever, almost always on the spot;
Tinsley's slows are often telling, though they sometimes catch it hot.
But however good their trundling, pitch or pace, or break or spin,
Still the monarch of all bowlers, to my mind, was Alfred Mynn.

William Jeffrey Prowse (1836–70)
Alfred Mynn

84 For cricket affords to a race of professionals a merry and abundant, though rather a laborious livelihood, from the time that the May-Fly is up to the time the first pheasant is down.

James Pycroft (1813–95)
The Cricket Field, 1851

85 Cricket is a habit you acquire for life.

Dilip Ramkissoon
New York Times, 31 July 1977

86   A good batsman is a wizard to watch. He dances down the wicket to meet the ball and places it just where he wants it to go.
Alex Reddin
New York Times, 31 July 1977

87   Minor counties cricketers are not all failed first-class cricketers. They may be professional people who have chosen a more financially rewarding career.
Neil Riddell
Sunday Telegraph, 12 March 1989

88   Making swift decisions on the field is the easy part; the tough part is explaining your decisions afterwards.
John Sheppard
Sunday Times, 23 April 1989

89   Try explaining cricket to an intelligent foreigner. It is far harder than explaining Chomsky's generational grammar.
Lord Snow
Jonathon Green, *A Dictionary of Contemporary Quotations*, 1982

90   IN AFFECTIONATE REMEMBRANCE
of
ENGLISH CRICKET
Which died at the Oval
29th August 1882
Deeply lamented by a large circle
of Sorrowing Friends and
Acquaintances
R.I.P.
N.B.– The body will be cremated,
and the ashes taken to Australia.
Sporting Times, 1882

91   Neither of us were worried who got the wickets as long as we were in our favourite position–our feet up, watching England play.
Brian Statham (on his partnership with Fred Trueman)
Observer, 'Sayings of the Week', 9 April 1989

92   Cricket of late years has become exceedingly fashionable, being much countenanced by the nobility and gentlemen of fortune, who frequently join in the diversion.
Joseph Strutt (1749–1802)
The Sports and Pastimes of the People of England, 1801, Bk. II, Ch. III, XIX

93   Personally, I have always looked on cricket as organized loafing.
William Temple (1881–1944)
Attributed

94   I dunno. Maybe it's that tally-ho lads attitude. You know, there'll always be an England, all that Empire crap they dish out. But I never could cop Poms.
Jeff Thomson
Observer, 'Sayings of the Week', 26 October 1987

95   Whatever great changes cricket may have undergone during the past century, it remained exactly as it is today in one respect – the start was delayed by rain.
Ben Travers
94 Declared: Cricket Reminiscences, 1981, Ch. 1

96   Like all cricket devotees I have many, many times shared with all around me that infectious, 'breathless hush' tension as a batsman, however well-set, however self-possessed, has to face up to the obligation of scoring that hundredth run.
Ben Travers
Ibid., Ch. 2

97   Fast bowling isn't hard work, it's horse work.
Fred Trueman
Jonathon Green, *A Dictionary of Contemporary Quotations*, 1982

98   People started calling me 'Fiery' because 'Fiery' rhymes with 'Fred' just like 'Typhoon' rhymes with 'Tyson'.
Fred Trueman
Private Eye, No. 522, 11 February 1983

99   That was a tremendous six: the ball was still in the air as it went over the boundary.
Fred Trueman
Private Eye, No. 588, 29 June 1984

100   That's what cricket is all about – two batsmen pitting their wits against one another.
Fred Trueman
Private Eye, No. 619, 6 September 1985

101 He's doing the best he can do – he's making the worst of a bad job.

Fred Truman, BBC Radio 3
Private Eye, No. 723, 1 September 1989

102 All winning captains are good captains – until they lose.

Derek Underwood
Beating the Bat, 1975, Ch. 7

103 When bowling to players of international class, I feel they don't have basic weaknesses but basic strengths; by avoiding their strengths one can often impart a superiority.

Derek Underwood
Deadly Down Under, 1980, Ch. 9

104 I never mind if I lose the toss, so long as I win the test.

Ajit Wadekar
C.D. Clark, *The Record-Breaking Sunil Gavaskar*, 1980, Ch. 7

105 A wicketkeeper should be judged by what he does and not what he fails to do.

E.M. Wellings
Vintage Cricketers, 1983, Ch. 9

106 Certainly I am told you can play cricket better after a marijuana cigarette than after a couple of pints of beer.

Lord Wigoder
The Times, 1 January 1987

107 Compared with techniques associated with other sports, fast bowling is a very unnatural thing . . . cricket is basically a sideways-on game, with batsman and bowler at an angle of ninety degrees to each other.

Bob Willis
Fast Bowling, 1984, Ch. 2

108 [As England captain] there is always a honeymoon period. It lasts until you lose.

Bob Willis
The Times, 28 July 1987

109 I am working very hard on this relaxation business.

Graeme Wood (Test opening bat)
Sydney Morning Herald, 'Sayings of the Week', 13 July 1985

21 CROQUET

1   Whence Croquet sprang to benefit the earth,
    What happy garden gave the pastime birth,
    What cunning craftsman carved its graceful tools,
    Whose oral teachings fixed its equal rules,
    Sing, Jaques, then apostle of the game!
    If disyllabic is thy famous name
    Or if, as Frenchified, it is but one,
    By saying, 'Sing, John Jaques!' the trick is done.
    Mysterious Croquet! like my 'Little Star'
    Of infancy, 'I wonder what you are?'
    Owning new parent, yet here in no shame,
    Where all the honour would so gladly claim.

Anonymous

2   The clunk of ball against mallet is a lovely sound, just like ice cubes in a gin and tonic.

Anonymous
Sunday Times, 19 July 1987

3   That relatively few people know how to play croquet is not a sign of feebleness or futility but that few people can meet its challenge with any success.

Roger Bray
National Westminster Bank, *Croquet*, 1973, Introduction

4   Croquet is perhaps one of the most maligned of sports.

Roger Bray
Croquet, 1974, Introduction

5   Something like 50 000 US-made croquet sets are sold per year – and with them 50 000 conflicting sets of rules.

Jack Osborn
New York Times, 17 July 1978

6   Croquet combines the mental challenge of chess, in terms of strategy, with the physical skill of golf putting and billiards.

Jack Osborn
Ibid.

22 CURLING

1   Curling is simply lawn bowling on ice.
Anonymous

2   [Curling is] a slippery game but it makes you stand on your own two feet.
Anonymous
Robin Welsh, *Beginners Guide to Curling*, 1969, Ch. 19

3   Only fifty per cent of curling is about throwing the stone. Of the rest, much is about commitment, team spirit and 'pressure'.
Bob Cowan
Curling and the Silver Broom, 1985, 'The Pressure Game'

4   The legs are the kingpins of curling.
Ed Lukowich
The Skol Book of Curling, 1982, Section 3

5   When a member falls and is hurt, the rest shall not laugh but render him every assistance to enable him to regain his former erect position.
Peebles Club regulation of 1821
Robin Welsh, *Beginner's Guide to Curling*, 1969, Ch. 10

6   A modern curling stone is a thing of beauty, its smooth and polished surface made more beautiful by reflected shades of blue, red or grey.
Robin Welsh
Beginner's Guide to Curling, 1969, Ch. 2

7   Curling has been described as 'bowls on ice'. We prefer the description as 'curling on grass'.
Robin Welsh
Ibid., Ch. 13

8   There are keen golfers, keen shinty players, keen anglers. But only curlers are 'keen keen'.
Robin Welsh
Ibid., Ch. 29

23 CYCLING

See also 60 Motor Cycling

1   Whoop la, out of the way
    We come with lightning speed,
    There's nothing like the rattling gate
    On the flying velocipede.
    Anonymous
    Frederick Alderson, *Bicycling: A History*, 1972, Ch. 2

2   The bicycle is complementary to the steam engine, doing for the horseless individual what the steam engine does for the community.
Sir Max Beerbohm (1872–1956)
Frederick Alderson *Bicycling: A History*, 1972, Ch. 6

3   Unfortunately women's cycling in Britain isn't moving with anyone except the ostriches.
Lisa Brambani
Financial Times, 27 August 1988

4   The reason why the medical profession looks so favourably on the bicycle is that it is built in such a way that it is virtually impossible to strain yourself on it, unless you do something really silly.
Reg Harris with G. H. Bowden
Two Wheels to the Top, 1976, Ch. 11

5   There's no way you can be a world-class skier and a world-class cyclist at the same time. You'd need sixteen months in a year to do that.
Steve Hegg
New York Times, 2 August 1984

6   Suffering, as only a racing cyclist can.
Barry Hoban with J. Wilcockson
Watching the Wheels Go Round, 1981, Ch. 1

7   The Tour de France is comparable to ... the Tour de France. It is a unique competition.
Barry Hoban with J. Wilcockson
Ibid., Ch. 5

8   When I saw Fignon on the podium I knew he was disappointed. What could I say to him? What could he say to me? I would have been devastated to lose by eight seconds.

Greg Lemond (after winning the Tour de France)
Independent, 'Quotes of the Week', 29 July 1989

9   He's a favourite for the Tour de France – well an outsider anyway.

Phil Liggett
Private Eye, No. 696, 19 August 1988

10   To ride in an international 'Tour' is a dream that comes true to few, and when they do get a chance to ride they do it because it is a challenge – a mental rather than a physical challenge.

Chas Messenger
Where There's a Wheel, 1972, Ch. 8

11   Next week we'll be looking at the Tour de France – all those bicycles roaring through the countryside.

Andy Peebles
Private Eye, No. 563, 15 July 1983

12   Cyclists represent only one per cent of the traffic, but they account for ten per cent of the traffic deaths. We physicians call cyclists 'organ donors'.

Cheryl Winchell
Observer, 'Sayings of the Week', 19 March 1989

24   DARTS

1   There's only one way to go from this, sixty double ten or twenty twenty double top.

Eric Bristow
Private Eye, No. 677, 27 November 1987

2   A lot of the Royals watch darts. Princess Anne watches a lot of it on telly. It gives the game some pull in America and Canada.

Eric Bristow
Independent, 14 January 1989

3   Give me a choice between the most beautiful bird in the world
and the world championships and I know what I'd choose. Darts
every time, mate. Darts every time.

Eric Bristow
Independent, 'Quotes of the Week', 20 January 1990

4   A good darts player who can count can always beat a brilliant
player who can't.

Leighton Rees
John Samuel, *The Guardian Book of Sports Quotes*, 1985

5   There are those who reckon it [darts] has no place in a yuppie
society. But I think they've gone overboard in cleaning it up. Darts
is *about* pints, fags and blokes in cardigans.

Sid Waddell
Observer, 7 January 1990

6   It was an easy decision to turn pro. I was unemployed.

Jocky Wilson
Sunday Correspondent, 7 January 1990

7   If darts comes off TV for good, then I'm away to Japan to take
up sumo wrestling.

Jocky Wilson
Independent, 'Quotes of the Week', 13 January 1990

25 DECATHLON

1   In my sport you have to peak ten times.

Daley Thompson
Sunday Times, 11 October 1981

2   I love the decathlon for the way it brings out your character.

Daley Thompson
Sports Illustrated, 20 August 1984

26 DISCUS

1   If you find the Roman exercises tiring because you are used to Greek ways, try the swift ball where the excitement disguises the hard work or, if you prefer discus-throwing, by all means hurl the discus through the yielding air.

Horace (Quintus Horatius Flaccus 65–8 BC)
Satires, II, ii, 10

2   If you ever hurl a discus at the empty air, may it knock you to the ground like young Oebalides [Hyacinthus].

Ovid (43 BC–AD 17)
Ibid., 1. 589

3   There are only four guys in the country [USA] who know how to throw the discus . . . It can be as easy as driving a car, but it's a question of cultural priorities. In this society, you want to be working on your first million by the time you're twenty-five, not throwing a discus.

Mac Wilkins
New York Times, 17 June 1988

27 DIVING

1   The springboard . . . is the board of education . . . You must work with it, but you sure don't want to knock heads with it.

Hobie Billingslea
Rose Mary Dawson, *Diving for Teacher and Pupil*, 1966, Ch. 2

2   Diving is an exercise in which the diver's body has imparted to it a certain amount of energy and momentum and is then for a brief period effectively isolated from its surroundings.

Dr George Eaves
Diving: The Mechanics of Springboard and Firmboard Techniques, 1969, Introduction

3   The diver feels his movement as the centre of action. He *is* the picture he is painting.

Anne Ross Fairbanks
Teaching Springboard Diving, 1964, Ch. 1

4   Less than winning means I failed.

Greg Louganis
New York Times, 12 May 1987

5   I'd like to be remembered as being strong and graceful and bringing a sense of art into this sport.

Greg Louganis
New York Times, 15 September 1988

6   There's no such thing as a perfect dive. I reach towards it but I'll never attain it.

Greg Louganis
Independent, 'Quotes of the Olympic Games', 1 October 1988

7   With good practice [at high level diving] you can avoid killing yourself.

Elizabeth Mackay
The Times, 3 August 1978

8   Diving is a form of art, for a diver is in effect painting a visual picture for the spectator. The diver's body represents the artist's brush, his style and technique are the colouring, and the dive performed is the basic design.

Ronald F. O'Brien
Springboard Diving, 1968, Ch. 1

28   DRAG RACING

1   Some sports are slow and there is a lot of wasted time, but drag racing is always moving.

Don Garlits
New York Times, 17 July 1977

2   We're killing the equipment because we're running so fast.

Shirley Muldowney
New York Times, 9 July 1978

29 DRUGS

1   When I'm competing in a game and the only difference was the other guy was beating me because he was taking drugs then I have two choices—I stop or I take drugs as well.
Boris Becker
Sunday Correspondent, 21 January 1990

2   As long as I'm a drug-free zone, that's all I worry about.
Linford Christie
Independent, 'Quotes of the Olympic Games', 1 October 1988

3   While the vast majority of athletes would no more take drugs than jump off Beachy Head, there are cheats at the margins and they have to be weeded out.
Sebastian Coe
Independent, 'Quotes of the Week', 11 March 1989

4   It was clear that steroids were worth approximately a metre at the highest levels of sport.
Charlie Francis, Ben Johnson's coach
Independent, 'Quotes of the Week', 4 March 1989

5   You have to be suspicious when you line up against girls with moustaches.
Maree Holland
Sydney Morning Herald, 'Sayings of the Year', 31 December 1988

30 EQUESTRIANISM

See also 73 Racing
83 Showjumping

1   The horse is a great leveller and anyone who is concerned about his dignity would be well advised to keep away from horses. Apart from many other embarrassments there is, for instance, no more ridiculous sight than a horse performing its natural functions with someone in full dress uniform mounted on its back.
Duke of Edinburgh
New York Times, 5 August 1984

2   I ride horseback because I prize my sleep, my digestion and my think-trap.

Elbert Hubbard (1856–1915)
Notebook, 1927, p. 93

3   Dressage is the nearest thing to skating. But at the moment, as dressage competitions are constituted, you are watching only the equivalent of compulsory figures.

Jennie Loriston-Clarke
The Times, 3 July 1984

4   Dressage to music is the ultimate test. And it is not the sort of po-faced thing most people think of as dressage.

Jennie Loriston-Clarke
Ibid.

5   Horse racing may be the sport of kings, but with about half a million horses of assorted shapes and sizes trotting around the country, riding can almost be classed as a mass sport.

Laura Phillips
Daily Telegraph, 7 September 1985

6   The transition from riding a pony to riding a horse is difficult, because they're, of course, totally different animals.

Lucinda Prior-Palmer
John Samuel, *The Guardian Book of Sports Quotes*, 1985

7   Well could he ride, and often men would say
     That horse his mettle from the rider takes:
     Proud of Subjection, noble by the sway,
     What rounds, what bounds, what course what stop he makes!
     And controversy hence a question takes,
     Whether the horse by him became his deed,
     Or he his manage by the well-doing steed.

William Shakespeare (1564–1616)
A Lover's Complaint

8   A horse! a horse! my kingdom for a horse!

William Shakespeare (1564–1616)
Richard III, 1592–93, Act V, Sc. IV

9 We don't want our sport [equestrianism] to become like showjumping, where you always see the same few riders, and there is little chance for others to get into the big televized meetings.

Ian Stark
Independent, 1 November 1989

31 EXERCISE

See also 34 Fitness

1 I never take any exercise. I guard against it. Exercise has done a lot of damage to my friends.

Lord Armstrong
Brian Mitchell, *Running to Keep Fit*, 1984

2 Better to hunt in fields for health unbought,
   Than fee the doctor for a nauseous draught.
   The wise, for cure, on exercise depend;
   God never made his work for man to mend.

   John Dryden (1631–1700)
   Epistle to J. Driden of Chesterton, 1700

3 Exercise is bunk. If you are healthy, you don't need it: if you are sick, you shouldn't take it.

Henry Ford (1863–1947)
Attributed

4 The rich advantage of good exercise.

William Shakespeare (1564–1616)
King John, 1596–97, Act IV, Sc. II

5 The only possible form of exercise is to talk, not to walk.

Oscar Wilde (1854–1900)
Rudolf Flesch, *The Book of Unusual Quotations*, 1959

32 FENCING

1 Fencing is a conversation with foils.
Anonymous

2 The qualities required of the complete swordsman are, on the physical side, technique, speed and stamina; mentally, he must possess judgment, opportuneness; and morally, perseverance.
Léon Bertrand
The Fencer's Companion, 1935, Pt. 1, Sec. 1

3 After the [Commonwealth Federation's fencing] championships I will be broke so I have just got to win that gold medal to make it all worthwhile.
Pierre Harper
The Times, 4 July 1878

4 Fencing . . . is a sport of skill, not strength; that's why women can fence men.
Sherry Marcy
New York Times, 5 June 1978

5 The killer instinct is something I find very hard to summon up . . . I have to tell myself again that I really do *hate* the person I'm fencing against.
Linda Martin
The Times, 13 June 1984

6 The implications of a shrinking base [in the number of British fencers] are serious for top-level fencing. Without a strong base at grass roots, it will become almost impossible to win Olympic medals. The problem is that without Olympic medals, it may be too late to build grass roots.
Barry Paul
Financial Times, 10 September 1988

7   The New Theatre, which . . . is this day begun to be employed by the fencers to play prizes at. And here I came and saw the first prize I ever saw in my life: and it was between one Matthews, who did beat at all weapons, and one Westwicke, who was soundly cut several times both in the head and legs, that he was all over blood: and other deadly blows they did give and take in very good earnest, till Westwicke was in a most sad pickle. They fought at eight weapons, three bouts at each weapon. It was very well worth seeing, because I did till this day think that it has only been a cheat.
Samuel Pepys (1633–1703)
Diary, 1 June 1663

8   I would I had bestowed that time in the tongues that I have in fencing, dancing, and bear-baiting. O! had I but followed the arts!
William Shakespeare, (1564–1616)
Twelfth Night, 1599–60, Act I, Sc. III

9   When you are fencing well, it's a feeling of being in control, a feeling of extending yourself as far as you can, a one-pointedness.
Frederic Torzs
York Times, 5 June 1978

33   FISHING

1   Each beat is to be fished by one male and one female rod but not two males. A youth under eighteen may fish as a female.
Anonymous
Conditions of two beats on the River Naver

2   If the fish pulls you, you pull him.
Anonymous (reference to salmon fishing)

3   If you want to be happy for a day, get drunk. If you want to be happy for a week, get married. But if you want to be happy for life, go fishing.
Anonymous

4   Lord give me grace to catch a fish
    So bid that even I
When talking of it afterwards
    May never need to lie.

Anonymous

5   Old fishermen don't die – they just smell that way.

Anonymous

6   The trouble with fish is that they go on holiday the same time as most anglers do.

Anonymous

7   Salmon fishing is made up largely of beliefs.

Conrad Voss Bark
The Times, 19 September 1985

8   A rod twelve feet long and a ring of wire,
A winder and barrel, will help thy desire
In killing a Pike; but the forked stick,
With a slit and a bladder, – and that other fine trick,
Which our artists call snap, with a goose or a duck, –
Will kill two for one, if you have any luck.

Thomas Barker (fl. 1651)
The Art of Angling, 1657

9   When a Pike suns himself and a-frogging doth go,
The two-inched hook is better, I know,
Than the ord'nary snaring: but still I must cry,
When the Pike is at home, minde the cookery.

Thomas Barker (fl. 1651)
Ibid.

10   Immense, of fishy form and mind,
    Squamous, omnipotent, and kind;
And under that Almighty fin,
The littlest fish may enter in.
Oh! never fly conceals a hook,
Fish say in the Eternal Brook,
But more than mundane weeds are there,
And mud, celestially fair.

Rupert Brooke (1887–1915)
Heaven

11   Unfading moths, immortal flies,
    And the worm that never dies.
    And in that Heaven of all their wish,
    There shall be no more land, say fish.
Rupert Brooke (1887–1915)
Ibid.

12   Fishing is a kind of hunting by water, be it with nets, weels, baits, angling or otherwise, and yields all out as much pleasure to some men as dogs or hawks.
Robert Burton (1577–1640)
The Anatomy of Melancholy, Pt. II, Sec. II

13   And angling too, that solitary vice,
    Whatever Izaak Walton sings or says:
    The quaint old cruel coxcomb, in his gullet
    Should have a hook, and a small trout to pull it.
Lord Byron (1788–1824)
Don Juan, 1823, Canto 13, St. 106

14   Fishing, with me, has always been an excuse to drink in the daytime.
Jimmy Cannon
Jonathon Green, *A Dictionary of Contemporary Quotations*, 1982

15   That great fishpond, the sea.
Thomas Dekker (1572–1632)
The Honest Whore, 1604, Act I

16   If the people don't want me, that's all right. I've a lot of fishing to do.
Dwight D. Eisenhower (1890–1969)
C. Bingham, *Wit and Wisdom*, 1982

17   We get fishing-tackle and go many miles to a watering place to catch fish, and having caught one and learned the whole mystery, we still repeat the process for the same result, though perhaps the fish are thrown overboard at last.
Ralph Waldo Emerson (1803–82)
Journal, 10 July 1841

18   A hook's well lost, to catch a salmon.
Thomas Fuller (1654–1734)
Gnomologia, 1732, No. 216

19   An angler eats more than he gets.
Thomas Fuller (1654–1734)
Ibid., No. 579

20   Fishes follow the bait.
Thomas Fuller (1654–1734)
Ibid., No. 1548

21   In the deepest water is the best fishing.
Thomas Fuller (1654–1734)
Ibid., No. 2824

22   It is a silly fish, that is caught twice with the same bait.
Thomas Fuller (1654–1734)
Ibid., No. 2879

23   It is good fish, if it were but caught.
Thomas Fuller (1654–1734)
Ibid., No. 2936

24   It is good fishing, in troubled waters.
Thomas Fuller (1654–1734)
Ibid., No. 2937
(*See also* Henry *below*)

25   It is vain to cast your net, where there is no fish.
Thomas Fuller (1654–1734)
Ibid., No. 2966

26   Muddy waters are the fisherman's gain.
Thomas Fuller (1654–1734)
Ibid., No. 3491

27   Still he fisheth, that catcheth one.
Thomas Fuller (1654–1734)
Ibid., No. 4262

28   The bait hides the hook.
Thomas Fuller (1654–1734)
Ibid., No. 4403

29   That fish will soon be caught that nibbles at every bait.
Thomas Fuller (1654–1734)
Ibid., No. 4342

30   'Tis rare to find a fish, that will not some time or other bite.
Thomas Fuller (1654–1734)
Ibid., No. 5114

31   Venture a small fish to catch a great one.
Thomas Fuller (1654–1734)
Ibid., No. 5347

32   I would rather go home empty-handed after a day playing a dry fly than catch monsters with a deep-sunk lure dressed like a saloon-bar slut.
Max Hastings
Independent, 'Quote Unquote', 6 May 1989

33   The English nation . . . are naturally 'brothers of the angle'. This pursuit implies just that mixture of patience and pastime, of vacancy and thoughtfulness, of idleness and business, of pleasure and of pain, which is suited to the genius of an Englishman.
William Hazlitt (1778–1830)
Merry England

34   To fish in troubled waters.
Matthew Henry (1662–1714)
Commentaries, Psalm LX
(See also Walton *below)*

35   But now he hath well fisht and caught a frogge.
John Heywood (1506–65)
Proverbs, 1546, Pt. I, Ch. XI

36   Fish is cast away that is cast in drie pooles.
John Heywood (1506–65)
Ibid.

37   All is fish that comth to net.
John Heywood (1506–65)
Ibid.

38   I . . . recall the old delight of boyish days, in fishing through the ice. It was not a sport of a lofty order, but it had a pleasure in it for an unsophisticated youth, to whom the trout was an unknown animal, and the fly a curious thing to read about in 'The Complete Angler'.
Oliver Wendell Holmes (1809–94)
The Seasons, 1868

39   Fishing is an emotional and not a commercial employment.
Oliver Wendell Homes (1809–94)
Ibid.

40   The more worthless a man, the more fish he can catch.
E. W. Howe (1853–1937)
Country Town Sayings, 1911

41   There is no good fishing.
E. W. Howe (1853–1937)
Ibid.

42   Angle . . . An instrument to take fish, consisting of a rod, a line, and a hook.
Samuel Johnson (1709–84)
Dictionary of the English Language, 1755

43   Fly fishing may be a very pleasant amusement; but angling or float fishing I can only compare to a stick and a string, with a worm at one end and a fool at the other.
Samuel Johnson (1709–84)
Attributed

44   It is a good fish when it is gripped [caught].
James Kelly
Scottish Proverbs, 1721, I, No. 262

45   Of all the fish in the sea, herring is the king.
James Kelly
Ibid., O, No. 56

46   You never heard a fisher cry stinking fish.
James Kelly
Ibid., Y, No. 297

47   Every man, deep down, is a fisherman.
Stephen Leacock (1869–1944)
Rudolf Flesch, *The Book of Unusual Quotations*, 1959

48   Fishing is a delusion entirely surrounded by liars in old clothes.
Don Marquis (1878–1937)
Clifton Fadiman, *The American Treasury: 1455–1955*, 1955

49   If I'd lost it [a salmon], I might have been tempted to give up
fishing altogether and taken up something less stressful like
alligator wrestling.

George Melly
Punch, 25 September 1985

50   Always let your hook be hanging, where you least expect it
there will be a fish in the stream.

Ovid (43 BC–AD 17)
The Art of Love, III

51   The mullet knocks the suspended bait with his tail, and
gathers it when it falls.

Ovid (43 BC–AD 17)
On Sea Fishing

52   This day Mr Caesar told me a pretty experiment of his, of
angling with a minikin, a gut-string varnished over, which keeps it
from swelling and is beyond any hair for strength and
smallness – the secret I like mightily.

Samuel Pepys (1633–1703)
Diary, 18 March 1667

53   Give me mine angle, – we'll to the river: there,
     My music playing far off, I will betray
     Tawney-finn'd fishes, my bended hook shall pierce
     Their slimy jaws; and as I draw them up
     I'll think them every one an Antony,
     And say, Ah, ha! you're caught.

William Shakespeare (1564–1616)
Antony and Cleopatra, 1606–7, Act II, Sc. V

54   'Twas merry when
     You wager'd on your angling; when your diver
     Did hang a salt fish on his hook, which he
     With fervency drew up.

William Shakespeare (1564–1616)
Ibid.

55   Rude fishermen of Corinth.

William Shakespeare (1564–1616)
The Comedy of Errors, 1592–93, Act V, Sc. I

56 A man may fish with the worm that hath eat of a king, and eat of the fish that hath fed of that worm.
William Shakespeare (1564–1616)
Hamlet, 1599–1600, Act IV, Sc. III

57 If the young dace be a bait for the old pike, I see no reason, in the law of nature, but I may snap at him.
William Shakespeare (1564–1616)
Henry IV Pt. II, 1597–98, Act III, Sc. II

58 Bait the hook well; this fish will bite.
William Shakespeare (1564–1616)
Much Ado About Nothing, 1598–99, Act II, Sc. III

> 59 The pleasant'st angling is to see the fish
> Cut with golden oars the silver stream,
> And greedily devour the treacherous bait.
> William Shakespeare (1564–1616)
> *Ibid.*, Act III, Sc. I

> 60 The fishermen who walk upon the beach.
> Appear like mice.
> William Shakespeare (1564–1616)
> *King Lear*, 1605–6, Act IV, Sc. VI

> 61 How the finny subject of the sea
> These fishers tell the infirmities of men;
> And from their watery empire recollect
> All that may men approve or men detect! –
> Peace be at your labour, honest fishermen.
> William Shakespeare (1564–1616)
> *Pericles*, 1608–9, Act II, Sc. I

62 Then thou wilt starve, sure; for here's nothing to be got now-a-days unless thou can fish for 't.
William Shakespeare (1564–1616)
Ibid.

63 Here's a fish hangs in the net like a poor man's right in the law; 'twill hardly come out.
William Shakespeare (1564–1616)
Ibid.

64   I am angling now.
     Though you perceive me not how I give line.

William Shakespeare (1564–1616)
The Winter's Tale, 1610–11, Act I, Sc. II

65 Caught the water, though not the fish.

William Shakespeare (1564–1616)
Ibid., Act V, Sc. II

66 They say fish should swim thrice ... first it should swim in the sea ... then it should swim in butter, and at last, sirrah, it should swim in good claret.

Jonathan Swift (1667–1745)
Polite Conversation, 1738, Dialogue 2

67 He minded not his friends' advice
     But followed his own wishes;
     But one most cruel trick of his
     Was that of catching fishes.

Jane Taylor (1783–1824)
Little Fisherman

68 My own feeling is that fish do not feel pain, but I think they can feel panic.

Don Thomson
Observer, 'Sayings of the Week', 8 January 1984

69 Two honest and good-natured anglers have never met each other without crying out 'What luck?'

Henry van Dyke (1852–1933)
Fisherman's Luck

70 I have laid aside business, and gone fishing.

Izaak Walton (1593–1683)
The Compleat Angler, 5th ed., 1676, 'To all readers of this Discourse but especially to the honest Angler'

71 Angling may be said to be so much like the mathematics, that it can ne'er be fully learnt; at least not so fully, but that there will still be more new experiments left for the trial of other men that succeed us.

Izaak Walton (1593–1683)
Ibid.

72   As no man is born an artist, so no man is born an Angler.
Izaak Walton (1593–1683)
Ibid.

73   I shall stay with him [the reader] no longer than to wish him a
rainy evening to read this following Discourse; and that (if he be
an honest Angler) the East wind may never blow when he goes a
Fishing.
Izaak Walton (1593–1683)
Ibid.

74   I am, Sir, a Brother of the Angle.
Izaak Walton (1593–1683)
Ibid., Pt. I, Ch. I

75   Angling is somewhat like poetry, men are to be born so: I
mean, with inclinations to it, though both may be heightened by
discourse and practice, but he that hopes to be a good angler must
not only bring an inquiring, searching, observing wit; but he must
bring a large measure of hope and patience, and a love and
propensity to the art itself; but having once got and practised it,
then doubt not but angling will prove to be so pleasant, that it will
prove to be like virtue, a reward to itself.
Izaak Walton (1593–1683)
Ibid.

76   Sir Henry Wootton ... was also a most dear lover, and a
frequent practiser of the art of angling; of which he would say,
'twas an employment for his idle time, which was then not idly
spent: for angling was after tedious study, a rest to his mind, a
cheerer of his spirits, a diverter of sadness, a calmer of unquiet
thoughts, a moderator of passions, a procurer of contentedness;
and that it begat habits of peace and patience in those that
professed and practised it.
Izaak Walton (1593–1683)
Ibid.

77   An excellent angler, and now with God.
Izaak Walton (1593–1683)
Ibid., Ch. IV

78   You must enjoy worse luck sometime, or you will never make
a good angler.
Izaak Walton (1593–1683)
Ibid.

79   As inward love breeds outward talk,
The hound some praise, and some the hawk:
Some better pleas'd with private sport,
Use tennis, some a mistress court:
   But these delights I neither wish,
   Nor envy, while I freely fish.

Who hunts, doth oft in danger ride;
Who hawks, lures oft both far and wide;
Who uses games shall often prove
A loser, but who falls in love,
   Is fettered in fond Cupid's snare:
   My angle breeds me no such care.

Izaak Walton (1593–1683)
Ibid., Ch. V, 'The Angler's Song'

80   Of recreation there is none
So free as fishing is alone;
All other pastimes do no less
Than mind or body both possess:
   My hand alone my work can do,
   So I can fish and study too.

Izaak Walton (1593–1683)
Ibid.

81 No life so happy and so pleasant as the life of a well-governed angler; for when the lawyer is swallowed up with business, and the statesman is preventing or contriving plots, then we sit on cowslip-banks, hear the birds sing, and possess our selves in as much quietness as these silent silver streams, which we now see glide so quietly by us . . . We may say of angling, as Dr Boteler said of strawberries, doubtless God could have made a better berry, but doubtless God never did: and so (if I might be judge) God never did make a more calm, quiet, innocent recreation than angling.

Izaak Walton (1593–1683)
Ibid.

82 Fishing is an art, or, at least, it is an art to catch fish.

Izaak Walton (1593–1683)
Ibid.

83   This dish of meat is too good for any but anglers or very honest men.

Izaak Walton (1593–1683)
Ibid., Ch. VIII

> 84   O the gallant fisher's life,
>   It is the best of any,
>   'Tis full of pleasure, void of strife,
>   And 'tis beloved by many:
>   Other joys
>   Are but toys,
>   Only this
>   Lawful is,
>   For our skill
>   Breeds no ill,
>   But content and pleasure.
>
> Izaak Walton (1593–1683)
> *Ibid.*, Ch. XVI

85   I love any discourse of rivers, and fish and fishing, the time spent in such discourses passes away very pleasantly.

Izaak Walton (1593–1683)
Ibid., Ch. XVIII

86   Let the blessing of St Peter's Master be with mine . . . and upon all that are lovers of virtue; and dare trust in his providence, and be quiet, and go a-Angling.

Izaak Walton (1593–1683)
Ibid., Ch. XXI

87   Anglers, they be such honest, civil, quiet men.

Izaak Walton (1593–1683)
Ibid.

88   It is well known that fishes enjoy being fished. But I do feel that fishing is rather cruel to worms. Nobody who has seen a worm on a hook can honestly pretend that the poor creature is enjoying it.

Auberon Waugh
Private Eye, No. 576, 13 January 1984, 'Auberon Waugh's Diary'

89   Fishing, as the golden page of English literature testifies, is a meditative and retrospective pursuit.

H.G. Wells (1866–1946)
The History of Mr Polly, 1909, Ch. X, 1

34 FITNESS

See also 31 Exercise

---

1   Age is not any indication of fitness.
Sebastian Coe
The Times, 16 January 1986

2   I'm an overweight athlete rather than a fat slob.
Robbie Coltrane
Observer, 'Sayings of the Week', 19 April 1987

3   I know I'm really fit when my workmates tell me how ill I look.
Steve Cram
The Times, 22 September 1988

4   Our own history, perhaps better than the history of any other great country, vividly demonstrates the truth of the belief that physical vigour and health are essential accompaniments to the qualities of intellect and spirit on which a nation is built.
John F. Kennedy
Sports Illustrated, 16 July 1962

---

35 FOOTBALL (AMERICAN)

See also 36 Football (Association)
37 Football (Gaelic)
79 Rugby

---

1   I am going to hit the other man and he's going to hit me. That's the game. If somebody gets injured, that's an accident.
George Atkinson
New York Times, 9 January 1977

2   Rugby is a beastly game played by gentlemen; soccer is a gentleman's game played by beasts; football is a beastly game played by beasts.
Henry Blaha
Jonathon Green, *A Dictionary of Contemporary Quotations*, 1982

3   Sometimes I get so anxious I try to run before I catch the ball.
I'll get better, even if I have to switch to Crazy Glue.

Eddie Brown
New York Times, 27 September 1988

4   Joe Montana is not human. I don't want to call him a god, but
he's definitely somewhere in between.

Cris Collingswood
Independent, 'Quotes of the Week', 16 December 1989

5   There is a function of a quasi religious nature performed by a
few experts but followed in spirit by the whole university world,
serving indeed as a symbol to arouse in the students and in the
alumni certain congregate and hieratic emotions. I refer, of
course, to football.

Charles Horton Cooley
Rudolf Flesch, *The Book of Unusual Quotations*, 1959

6   You've got to explode through the tackle; you've got to learn to
take impulsion from the hip.

Roger Craig
The Times, 21 January 1989

7   Sure, I've been hit, but I think the way I play is more careful
than just sitting back in the pocket, where you are taking hits from
guys weighing 300 lb. I think that those might hurt a little bit more
than the ones I take from guys who are usually around 190 lb.

Randall Cunningham
Sunday Times, 6 August 1989

8   You can learn more character on the two-yard line than you
can anywhere in life.

Paul Dietzel
Sports Illustrated, 26 November 1962

9   A leading American football player was asked on television
whether he preferred Astroturf or grass. He replied, 'I don't
know, man, I've never smoked Astroturf.'

Tim Fell
John Samuel, *The Guardian Book of Sports Quotes*, 1985

10   I am glad that thousands of fine Americans can spend this Saturday afternoon 'knocking each other down' in a spirit of clean sportsmanship and keen competition instead of assaulting Pentagon soldiers or policemen with their 'peace' placards and filthy words.

Gerald Ford
Attributed

11   Pro football is like nuclear warfare. There are no winners, only survivors.

Frank Gifford
Sports Illustrated, 4 July 1960

12   Why can't a football player git a picture taken that don't make him look like he wuz wanted fer somethin'?

Frank McKinney Hubbard (1868–1930)
New Sayings By Abe Martin, 1917

13   Football occupies the same relation to education that a bullfight does to farming.

Frank McKinney Hubbard (1868–1930)
Epigrams, 1923

14   American football is not so much a sport as a way of strife. It might best be described as rugby league with knobs on, or feinting by numbers.

Doug Ibbotson
Sporting Scenes, 1980, Ch. 6

15   Football season is the only time of the year when girls whistle at men in sweaters.

Robert Q. Lewis
Clifton Fadiman, *The American Treasury: 1455–1955*, 1955

16   Some people try to find things in this game that don't exist. Football is two things. It's blocking and tackling.

Vince Lombardi
Barbara Rowes, *The Book of Quotes*, 1979

17   Win a team's heart and they'll follow you anywhere, do the impossible for you.

Vince Lombardi
Attributed

18   American football? It's a sick game, that's all. Big guys trying
to beat the crap out of each other. If I could play golf just as well,
I'd do it for a living. It's no fun waking up on Monday morning and
you can't get out of bed. Golfers don't have that problem.
Jim McMahon (quarterback of the Chicago Bears)
The Times, 2 August 1986

19   Defence is people . . . the best defences in football have less
to do with design than with players.
John Madden
New York Times, 6 January 1977

20   I've lost six pounds this past week, but that's like throwing a
deck chair off the *Queen Mary*.
Bill Parcells, nicknamed Big Tuna
Observer, 1 February 1987

21   I resigned as coach because of illness and fatigue. The fans
were sick and tired of me.
John Ralston
John Samuel, *The Guardian Book of Sports Quotes*, 1985

22   American attitudes toward football demonstrate a forceful
need to define, limit and conventionalize the symbolism of
violence in sports.
David Riesman and Revel Denny
American Quarterly, 'Football in America: A Study in Cultural Diffusion', 1951

23   Football doesn't build character. It gets rid of weak ones.
Darrell Royal
Jerry Tarkanian and William E. Warren, *Winning Basketball Systems*, 1981, Ch. 2

24   The football critic pretends to hate bad play, but he loves it.
What he really hates is good play, for good play makes his services
unnecessary. His long suit is disgust, and vulgar abuse is always
trumps.
John D. Sheridan
Clifton Fadiman, *The American Treasury: 1455–1955*, 1955

25   In this game all you need is speed, strength and an ability to
recognize pain immediately.
Reggie Williams
John Samuel, *The Guardian Book of Sports Quotes*, 1985

26   Fans are having fun and players have fun, so why can't coaches too?

Sam Wyche
New York Times, 26 September 1988

36   FOOTBALL (ASSOCIATION)

See also 35 Football (American)
37 Football (Gaelic)

1   Like sex, the movements in football are limited and predictable.

Peter Ackroyd
The Times, 21 June 1982

2   This is what life is about, not playing ninety minutes as a footballer. My life is seventy years, football is just a part of it. I think this issue is going completely over the top.

Martin Allen (on being fined two weeks' wages by his club for missing a match to be with his wife at the birth of their first child)
The Times, 14 March 1989

3   Getting sacked is just part of the football scene.

Malcolm Allison
Observer, 'Sayings of the Week', 12 October 1980

4   A lot of hard work went into this defeat.

Malcolm Allison
Independent, 'Quotes of the Week', 9 September 1989

5   Football is a gentleman's game played by hooligans, and rugby a hooligan's game played by gentlemen.

Anonymous
(See also Tony Mason *below)*

6   I cannot consider the game of football as being at all gentlemanly. It is a game which the common people of Yorkshire are particularly partial to, the tips of their shoes being heavily shod with iron: and frequently death has been known to ensue from the severity of the blows inflicted thereby.

Anonynmous
Eton, by an Etonian, 1831

7   The sturdy plowman, lusty, strong and bold
    Overcometh the winter with driving the football
    Forgetting labour and many a grievous fall.
Anonymous, early sixteenth century
William J. Baker, *Sports in the Western World*, 1982, Ch. 4

8   No team should look further than its next match.
Anonymous

9   Of course, we are all in the entertainment business.
Ossie Ardiles
The Times, 10 February 1990

10   A manager is one more among ourselves. But I have said that my players must never forget that I am the one, and they are the more.
Xavier Ascargorta
Sunday Times, 11 January 1987

11   Women should be in the kitchen, the discotheque and the boutique, but not in football.
Ron Atkinson, BBC2
Independent, 'Quotes of the Week', 3 June 1989

12   When the ball comes out of the sky, we'll start to play. If we keep it on the floor we'll win, if we don't we won't.
Alan Ball
The Times, 31 January 1987

13   I always wanted to be the greatest player and got somewhere near to that. Now I want to be the greatest coach and manager in the country.
Alan Ball
Independent, 19 October 1989

14   Next to hooligans, the people I'd most like to lose interest in football are kit manufacturers.
Patrick Barclay
Guardian, 7 September 1985

15   I'd have to be a superman to do some of the things I'm supposed to have done . . . I've been in six different places at six different times.
George Best
Private Eye, No. 565, 12 August 1983

16   I don't know what's happened to Total Football, I never quite understood what people meant by the term.

Danny Blanchflower
Sunday Times, 10 July 1977

17   The great fallacy is that the game is first and last about winning. It is nothing of the kind. The game is about glory, it is about doing things in style and with a flourish, about going out and beating the lot, not waiting for them to die of boredom.

Danny Blanchflower
Attributed

18   Football is not a logical game.

Mihir Bose
Sunday Times, 7 December 1986

19   A footballer can never plan his career.

Liam Brady
Sunday Times, 23 November 1986

20   John Motson: Well, Trevor, what does this substitution mean tactically?
Trevor Brooking: Well, Barnes has come off and Rocastle has come on . . .

Trevor Brooking
Private Eye, No. 727, 27 October 1989

21   Parents see soccer as a squeaky-clean sport. In other sports, people are imprisoned in one position for life – once a quarter-back, always a quarterback – soccer personifies the American ideal of freedom.

Al Calone
Independent, 'Quotes of the Week', 23 September 1989

22   All I know most surely about morality and the obligations of man, I owe to football.

Albert Camus (1913–60)
Attributed

23   I wish I could play music and talk the way I feel football.

Bobby Charlton
The Times, 19 September 1972

24   I won't die at a football match. I might die being dragged down the River Tweed by a giant salmon but not at a football match.

Jack Charlton
Independent, 'Quotes of the Week', 26 November 1988

25   There is no such thing as a football hooligan. They are all just hooligans.

Brian Clough
Observer, 'Sayings of the Week', 21 September 1980

26   If the African nations ever succeeded in their plan for one British team in the World Cup, I'd vote Tory. That is how serious it is. I ask you, a load of spear throwers trying to dictate our role in world football.

Brian Clough
Observer, 'Sayings of the Week', 15 February 1987

27   Nottingham Forest are having a bad run . . . they've lost six matches now without winning.

David Coleman
Private Eye, No. 555, 25 March 1983

28   Alf Ramsay was being crucified by the press when I started and now I am about to leave it is Bobby Robson's turn.

Ted Croker
Independent, 'Quotes of the Week', 11 February 1989

29   There was a problem of balance but it was the same for both sides.

George Curtis
Sunday Today, 1 February 1987

30   You know, the Brazilians aren't as good as they used to be, or as they are now.

Kenny Dalglish
Private Eye, No. 718, 23 June 1989

31   Lukic saved with his foot which is all part of the goalkeeper's arm.

Barry Davis
Private Eye, No. 660, 3 April 1987

32   You can't buy instant success in football because it's . . . a team game.

John Deacon
The Times, 20 February 1987

33   Footeballe is to be utterly abiected of al noble men, wherein is nothing but beastly furie and extreme violence; whereof procedeth hurte, and consequently rancour and malice do remaine with them that be wounded; whereof it is to be put in perpetuall silence.

Sir Thomas Elyot (1490?–1546)
The Gouvenour, 1531

34   If you really want something, you can get it. Your body will follow your mind.

Justin Fashanu
Guardian, 21 October 1989

35   Hearts 2 Motherwell 0. A good fight back there by Motherwell who were 2–0 down at one stage.

Paddy Feeny, BBC World Service
Private Eye, No. 701, 28 October 1988

36   You care, care about the people who support you. At Manchester United you become one of them, you think like a supporter, suffer like a supporter.

Alex Ferguson
Observer, 1 October 1989

37   He doesn't need a medical. Colin Hendry can play football without legs. He is built like a young bull.

Bill Fox
Sunday Telegraph, 12 November 1989

38   I'd rather have a guy take me to a football match and have a drink afterwards than go to bed with someone.

Samantha Fox
The Times, 1 January 1987

39   I still get as big a thrill scoring goals as I did when I had four in a match when I was a sixteen-year-old at Birmingham.

Trevor Francis
Sunday Times, 4 February 1990

40   All are fellows at football.
Thomas Fuller (1654–1734)
Gnomologia, 1732, No. 498

41   Two to one is odds at foot-ball.
Thomas Fuller (1654–1734)
Ibid., No. 5337

> 42   Where *Covent-garden*'s famous Temple stands,
>   That boasts the Work of *Jones'* immortal Hands;
>   Columns, with plain Magnificence, appear,
>   And graceful Porches lead along the Square:
>   Here oft' my Course I bend, when lo! from far,
>   I spy the Furies of the Foot-ball War:
>   The 'Prentice quits his shop, to join the Crew,
>   Encreasing Crouds the flying Game Pursue.
>   Thus, as you roll the Ball o'er snowy Ground,
>   The gath'ring Globe augments with ev'ry Round;
>   But whither shall I run? the Throng draws nigh,
>   The Ball now Skims the Street, now soars on high;
>   The dext'rous Glazier strong returns the Bound,
>   And gingling Sashes on the Pent-house sound.
> John Gay (1685–1732)
> *Trivia*, 1716, Bk. II

43   A young man of real ability would have to think twice about a career in English soccer management. Who would be judging his work? Amateurs, mostly.
Johnny Giles
Sunday Times, 9 August 1981

44   He hit the post, and after the game people will say, well he hit the post.
Jimmy Greaves
Private Eye, No. 602, 11 January 1985

45   There are only two basic situations in football. Either you have the ball or you haven't.
Ron Greenwood
John Samuel, *The Guardian Book of Sports Quotes*, 1985

46   Celtic manager David Hay still has a fresh pair of legs up his sleeve.
John Greig
Private Eye, No. 648, 17 October 1986

47   Football's not like an electric light. You can't just flick the button and change from slow to quick.
John Greig
Private Eye, No. 678, 11 December 1987

48   The game finely balanced with Celtic well on top.
John Greig, Radio Scotland
Private Eye, No. 726, 13 September 1989

49   There's never a good time to score an own goal against yourself.
John Greig
Private Eye, No. 727, 27 October 1989

50   If a week's a long time in politics it's an equinox in football.
Stuart Hall
Private Eye, No. 654, 9 January 1987

51   This is the first time Denmark has ever reached the World Cup Finals, so this is the most significant moment in Danish history.
John Helm
Private Eye, No. 640, 27 June 1986

52   What would Scotland be like without football? English.
Tony Higgins
Sunday Times, 30 August 1987

53   We will never again in this country [UK] see a club pay £1 million for a player.
Peter Hill-Wood
Observer, 'Sayings of the Week', 19 September 1982

54   These days I need ten minutes' notice to score.
Joe Jordan
Independent, 'Quotes of the Week', 18 February 1989

55   Bobby Robson must be thinking of throwing some fresh legs on.
Kevin Keegan
Private Eye, No. 664, 29 May 1987

56   The organization of football is a reflection of our national life.
Professor George W. Keeton
The Soccer Club Secretary, 1951, Ch. VI

57   Football is essentially a public activity, of great social importance.
Professor George W. Keeton
Ibid., Ch. VIII

58   Dickie Davis: What's he going to be telling his team at half-time, Denis?
     Denis Law: He'll be telling them that there are forty-five minutes left to play.

Denis Law
Private Eye, No. 560, 3 June 1983

59   Last time we got a penalty away from home, Christ was still a carpenter.
Lennie Lawrence
Sunday Correspondent, 29 October 1989

60   Some of these players never dreamed they would be playing in a Cup Final at Wembley, but here they are fulfilling those dreams.
Laurie McMenemy
Private Eye, No. 522, 18 December 1981

61   The goal was scored a little bit by the hand of God, another bit by the head of Maradona.
Diego Maradona
Observer, 'Sayings of the Year', 28 December 1986

62   Soccer in England is a grey game, played on grey days, watched by grey people.
Rodney Marsh
Observer, 'Sayings of the Week', 18 September 1977

63   The [North American Soccer] League is no longer saturated with English players because those who come here [USA] now have to be of a much higher calibre. It's true the English game is perhaps more productive, but I want freedom, flair. That's show business, isn't it?
Rodney Marsh
New York Times, 27 May 1979

64   All a manager has to do is keep eleven players happy – the eleven in the reserves. The first team are happy because they're the first team.
Rodney Marsh
Jonathon Green, *A Dictionary of Contemporary Quotations*, 1982

65   If rugby football was a hooligan's game played by gentlemen, then association was a gentlemen's game not only played by hooligans but also watched by them.

Tony Mason
Association Football and English Society, 1863–1915, Introduction.
(See also Anonymous *above)*

66   Football is a great art to be enjoyed. It is universal, exciting, it demands great skill, tenacity and courage in adversity.

Robert Maxwell
Observer, 5 May 1985

67   In Scotland football hooliganism has been met by banning alcohol from grounds but in England this solution has been circumnavigated.

Wallace Mercer
Private Eye, No. 576, 13 January 1984

68   Many supporters say they wouldn't stand for all-seater stadiums.

Guy Michelmore, BBC1
Private Eye, No. 718, 23 June 1989

69   Football is business. And business is business.

Rinus Michels
Jonathon Green, *A Dictionary of Contemporary Quotations*, 1982

70   The World Cup–truly an international event.

John Motson
Private Eye, No. 640, 27 June 1986

71   The game is balanced in Arsenal's favour.

John Motson
Private Eye, No. 655, 23 January 1987

72   Soccer is life itself for a Scot.

Shuggy Murney
Sydney Morning Herald, 'Sayings of the Week', 7 December 1985

73   Now listen boys, I'm not happy with our tackling. We're hurting them but they keep getting up.

Jimmy Murphy (when managing Wales in a match against England)
Independent, 18 March 1989

74   Don't try to break the bloody net, pass the ball into it.
Billy Nicholson
Attributed

75   With the very last kick of the game, Bobby McDonald scored with a header.
Alan Parry
Private Eye, No. 501, 27 February 1981

76   The FA Cup has a miraculous effect on injuries – better than any physiotherapist.
Jack Pearce
Independent, 19 November 1988

77   I don't care how close you are to me, if you play for the other team I want to kill you.
Pelé (Edson Orantes di Nascimento)
New York Times, 3 July 1977

78   The street being full of footballs.
Samuel Pepys (1633–1703)
Diary, 3 January 1664–5

79   If I want to be happy I switch on videos of Luton Town's midfield players playing like basketball players, interchanging with movement, and all of a sudden I can enjoy life again.
David Pleat
Guardian, 27 October 1989

80   Managers get too much of the praise and too much of the blame.
Sir Alf Ramsey
Independent, 22 October 1988

81   We need to treat football as a cultural industry.
Dr Steve Redhead of Manchester Polytechnic
Guardian, 28 October 1989

82   I should have forgotten all about trying to play more controlled, attractive football and settled for a real bastard of a team.
Don Revie
Guardian, 3 April 1989

83   Of course I'm against Sunday soccer. It'll spoil my Saturday nights.

John Ritchie
John Samuel, *The Guardian Book of Sports Quotes*, 1985

84   Anyone who can't score from a penalty needs shooting.

Graham Rix
Observer, 'Sayings of the Week', 18 May 1980

85   Football's a game of skill . . . we kicked them a bit and they kicked us a bit.

Graham Roberts
Private Eye, No. 557, 22 April 1983

86   Don't tell me that unruly players don't incite crowd trouble because I've seen it happen.

Bobby Robson
Observer, 'Sayings of the Week', 29 August 1982

87   I do want to play the long ball, and I do want to play the short ball. I think long and short balls is what football is all about.

Bobby Robson
Private Eye, No. 556, 8 April 1983

88   As far as I'm concerned, there is no job other than being England manager that is worth considering.

Bobby Robson
The Times, 16 June 1984

89   With Maradona, even Arsenal would have won it [the 1986 World Cup].

Bobby Robson
The Times, 1 January 1987

90   We are close to having a side capable of taking on the world.

Bobby Robson
Observer, 'Sayings of the Week', 24 August 1988

91   You have to have a broad back, take criticism on the chin and soldier on.

Bobby Robson
Independent, 'Quotes of the Week', 22 October 1988

92   I cannot play fifty-seven players in an England team, but I would have to do that to accommodate everyone I'm told to pick.
Bobby Robson
Daily Telegraph, 17 November 1988

93   Just because we're England, it doesn't mean we have a divine right to go all over the world beating other countries.
Bobby Robson
Observer, 'Sayings of the Week', 20 November 1988

94   Lovers of football are the most conservative people in the world, and real lovers of football are necessarily a little bigoted where reform is concerned.
Routledge's *Handbook of Football,* 1867

95   It is a good plan, if it can be previously so arranged, to have one side with striped jerseys of one colour, say red; and the other with another, say blue. This prevents confusion and wild attempts to run after and wrest the ball from your neighbour. I have often seen this done, and heard the invariable apology—'I beg your pardon. I thought you were on the opposite side.'
Ibid.

96   Soccer has elements of both ballet and chess.
Vidal Sassoon
Observer, 10 August 1979

97   Yet, in a hundred scenes, all much the same,
    I know that weekly half a million men
Who never actually played the game,
    Hustling like cattle herded in a pen,
        Look on and shout,
    While two-and-twenty hirelings hack a ball about.
Sir Owen Seaman (1861–1936)
People's Sport

98   Am I so round with you, as you with me,
That like a football you do spurn me thus?
You spurn me hence, and he will spurn me hither:
If I last in this service you must case me in leather.
William Shakespeare (1564–1616)
Comedy of Errors, 1592–93, Act II, Sc. I

99   You base football player.
William Shakespeare (1564–1616)
King Lear, 1605–6, Act I, Sc. IV

100   Some people think football is a matter of life and death. I don't like that attitude. I can assure them it is much more serious than that.
Bill Shankly
Jonathon Green, *A Dictionary of Contemporary Quotations,* 1982

101   Of course a player can have sexual intercourse before a match and play a blinder. But if he did it for six months he'd be a decrepit old man. It takes away the strength from the body.
Bill Shankly
John Samuel, *The Guardian Book of Sports Quotes,* 1985

102   Enjoy it while you can. There is nothing like playing but it doesn't last for ever.
Bill Shankly
Independent, 11 February 1989

103   Foot-ball ... was formerly much in vogue among the common people of England, though of late years it seems to have fallen into disrepute, and is but little practised.
Joseph Strutt (1749–1802)
The Sports and Pastimes of the People of England, 1801, Bk. II, Ch. III, XIII

104   When a match at foot-ball is made, two parties, each containing an equal number of competitors, take the field, and stand between two goals, placed at the distance of eighty or a hundred yards the one from the other. The goal is usually made with two sticks driven into the ground, about two or three feet apart ... The object of each party is to drive [the ball] through the goal of their antagonists, which being achieved the game is won. The abilities of the performers are best displayed in attacking and defending the goals; and hence the pastime was more frequently called a goal at foot-ball than a game at football. When the exercise becomes exceeding violent, the players kick each other's shins without the least ceremony, and some of them are overthrown at the hazard of their limbs.
Joseph Strutt (1749–1802)
Ibid

105   It's tight, taut and muscular. Bobby Moore's posterior comes top of our Girls' Bottom League.

Sun
John Samuel, *The Guardian Book of Sports Quotes*, 1985

106   I really do believe that it's not whether you win or lose that matters, but how you play the game. And, come the next century, football can only succeed if it is based on those kind of ideals, rather than the modern-day, Yuppie tabloid philosophy of wanting success yesterday.

Gordon Taylor
Sunday Telegraph, 3 December 1989

107   Professional football is such a cut-throat business that when things are not going right fifty per cent of the people are quite pleased and the other fifty per cent couldn't give a damn.

Graham Taylor
Sunday Telegraph, 26 March 1989

108   Well I think Arsenal will either win or lose the championship this year.

Graham Taylor, ITV
Private Eye, No. 716, 26 May 1989

109   If you win a game you are a genius; if you lose one you are worse than useless. There is no middle road.

John Toshack as manager of Real Madrid
Independent, 18 October 1989

110   I'm sweating more on the bench than some of the players on the field.

John Toshack
Sunday Telegraph, 'Quotes 1989', 24 December 1989

111   There's no fun in soccer any more. It's all deadly serious. We'll end up playing in cemeteries.

Terry Venables
John Samuel, *The Guardian Book of Sports Quotes*, 1985.

112   There is a fine line between bravery and suicide.

Terry Venables
Independent, 12 November 1988

113   Replacing the England manager to put the game to rights is about as useful as giving a cup of tea to someone who is bleeding to death.

Allen Wade (letter to Ken Jones)
Independent, 22 October 1988

114   Talk about a football pitch! Well, this one eclipsed any I ever heard of or saw. I could not venture to say what shape it was, but it was bounded by back yards about two-thirds of the area, and the other portion was – I was going to say a ditch, but I think an open sewer would be more appropriate. We could not decide who won the game, for when the ball was not in the back gardens it was in the ditch, and that was full of the loveliest material that could possibly be.

E. Watkins (first secretary of Arsenal Football Club describing their first match against Eastern Wanderers at Milwall in December 1886)
William Lownes, *The Story of Football*, 1952, Ch. VII

115   What they say about footballers being ignorant is rubbish. I spoke to a couple yesterday and they are quite intelligent.

Raquel Welch
John Samuel, *The Guardian Book of Sports Quotes*, 1985

116   The higher you go in football, the less you can afford to lose possession.

Ray Wilkins
Sunday Correspondent, 12 November 1989

117   I am a firm believer that if you score one goal the other team have to score two to win.

Howard Wilkinson
Private Eye, No. 570, 21 October 1983

118   A team evolves, like a child does.

Howard Wilkinson
Sunday Correspondent, 7 January 1990

119   Football is a harsh mistress.

Barrie Williams
Independent, 'Quotes of the Week', 4 February 1989

120   I know more about football than politics.

Harold Wilson
John Samuel, *The Guardian Book of Sports Quotes*, 1985

121   Much [has] been said of the English spending their time on drinking, but these kinds of sports kept young men from so spending and wasting their time, for, after playing a good game of football . . . they would be more glad to go to bed than to visit the public house.
Sir Watkin Wynne
Athletic News, 22 June 1881

37   GAELIC FOOTBALL

See also 35 Football (American)
36 Football (Association)

1   Gaelic football is one of the great amateur games in the world . . . The game is Gaelic in its very essence. All the consequences of this Gaelic nature combine to give it character.
Joe Lennon
Coaching Gaelic Football, 1964, Conclusion

2   One of the great features of Gaelic football is the high catching skills of the midfield players.
Paddy Moriarty
Observer, 15 October 1989

38   FOX HUNTING

1   He thought at heart like courtly Chesterfield.
Who, after a long chase o'er the hills, dales, brushes,
And what not, though he rode beyond all price,
Ask'd next day, 'if men ever hunted *twice*?'
Lord Byron (1788–1824)
Don Juan, 1823, Canto 14, St. 35

2   And though the fox he follows may be tamed,
A mere fox-follower is never reclaim'd.
William Cowper (1731–1800)
Conversation, 1782

3   There is a field through which I often pass,
Thick overspread with moss and silky grass . . .
Where oft the bitch-fox hides her hapless brood,
Reserved to solace many a neighbouring squire,
That he may follow them through brake and brier,
Contusion hazarding of neck or spine,
Which rural gentlemen call sport divine.

William Cowper (1731–1800)
The Needless Alarm, 1794

4   The fox knows much, but more he that catcheth him.

Thomas Fuller (1654–1734)
Gnomologia, 1732, No. 4544

5   D'ye ken John Peel with his coat so gray?
D'ye ken John Peel at the break of day?
D'ye ken John Peel when he's far, far away
With his hounds and his horn in the morning?
'Twas the sound of his horn called me from my bed,
And the cry of his hounds has me oft-times led,
For Peel's view hollo would awaken the dead
Or a fox from his lair in the morning.

D'ye ken that bitch whose tongue is death?
D'ye ken her sons of peerless faith?
D'ye ken that a fox with his last breath
Cursed them all as he died in the morning?

John Woodcock Graves (1795–1886)
John Peel

6   For Fox Sake
Stop Hunting

Hunt Saboteurs' Association

7   What! Labour has just lost my vote. It's like telling people they can't follow the religion of their choice. If I want to hunt foxes, I will, and if I want to get my cat all groomed up to go rat hunting, I'll do that too.

Peter Janson (on the Australian Labour Party's anti-fox hunting policy)
Melbourne *Age*, 4 March 1982
Bill Wannan, *Great Aussie Quotes*, 1982

8   I have now learned by hunting, to perceive, that it is no diversion at all, nor ever takes a man out of himself for a moment: the dogs have less sagacity than I could have prevailed on myself to suppose; and the gentlemen often call to me not to ride over them. It is very strange, and very melancholy, that the paucity of human pleasures should persuade us ever to call hunting one of them.
Samuel Johnson (1709–84)
Johnsonian Miscellanies, 1897, Vol. I

9   When men grew shy of hunting stag,
    For fear the Law might try 'em,
The Car put up the average bag
    Of twenty dead *per diem.*
Then every road was made a rink
    For Coroners to sit on;
And so began, in skid and stink,
    The real blood-sport of Britain!
Rudyard Kipling (1865–1936)
Fox-Hunting, 1933

10   Ladies whose husbands love fox hunting are in a poor way.
Sir Walter Scott (1771–1832)
Journal, 17 March 1829

11   So then, men vaunt in vaine, which say they hunt the Foxe
    To kepe their neighbours poultry free, and to defend their
        flockes –
When they themselves can spoyle more profit in an houre
Than Reynard rifles in a yere, when he doth most devoure.
George Turberville (1540?–1610?)
The Noble Art of Venerie, 1575

12   It has been said that if foxes could vote, they'd vote Tory.
Geoffrey Wheatcroft (referring to the argument that foxes suffer less from fox hunting than they would from other methods of control, and the Labour Party's opposition to fox hunting)
Sunday Telegraph, 1 March 1987

13   The English country gentleman galloping after a fox – the unspeakable in full pursuit of the uneatable.
Oscar Wilde (1854–1900)
A Woman of No Importance, 1893, Act I

39 GLIDING

See also **44** Hang Gliding

1   Glider pilots keep it up longer.
Anonymous

2   The ability to stay aloft and even gain altitude without an engine makes soaring a most fascinating combination of nature, science and skill.
William T. Carter
Soaring: The Sport of Flying Sailplanes, 1974, Ch. 1

3   Gliding is probably the nearest we shall get to flying as the birds know it.
John Simpson
Tackle Gliding This Way, 1961, Ch. 1

40 GOLF

1   It took me seventeen years to get three thousand hits in baseball. I did it in one afternoon on the golf course.
Henry Aaron
Barbara Rowes, *The Book of Quotes,* 1979

2   And now to hole eight which is in fact, the eighth hole.
Peter Alliss
Private Eye, No. 605, 22 February 1985

3   A caddy is someone who accompanies the golfer and didn't see the ball either.
Anonymous

4   Different folks need different strokes.
Anonymous

5   Golf – hockey at the halt.
Anonymous
Sunday Telegraph, 6 October 1985

6   Everything about golf is getting bigger. The galleries, the prize money and the number of youngsters. I think you'll see the competitive life expectancy of golfers getting shorter.
George Archer
New York Times, 2 July 1978

7   The wit of man has never invented a pastime equal to golf for its healthful recreation, its pleasurable excitement, and its never ending source of amusement.
Lord Balfour (1848–1930)
Bob Chieger and Pat Sullivan, *The Book of Golf Quotations*, 1987

8   I am quite certain that there has never been a greater addition to the lighter side of civilization than that supplied by the game of golf.
Lord Balfour (1848–1930)
Ibid.

9   Maybe I should go to a sports shop and buy a trophy. That's the only way I'm going to get one.
Severiano Ballesteros
Norman Giller, *The Book of Golf Lists*, 1985

10   I look into their eyes, shake their hand, pat their back and wish them luck, but I am thinking, 'I am going to bury you.'
Severiano Ballesteros
Guardian, 14 October 1989

11   I am a golfer. I have played for twenty years but I have recently made a discovery. I *hate* it!
Rex Beach
Foreword to Alex J. Morrison, *A New Way to Better Golf*, 1932

12   The alligator thing was nothing big. I just saw a little five-foot alligator once near a water hole in Florida and flipped it over by its tail. That's easy. But the guy I was playing with made it sound like I wrestled it.
Andy Bean
New York Times, 17 June 1978

13   It is hard to enjoy a thrashing but every good man is tested in the crucible of humiliation ... Unfortunately in golf there are more times like this than others.
Chip Beck
Guardian, 14 October 1989

14   It's not in support of cricket but as an earnest protest against golf.
Sir Max Beerbohm (1872–1956) (on giving a shilling to W. G. Grace's testimonial)
Attributed

15   Golf is the most straightforward, honest competition in the world. There are no substitutes allowed, the game doesn't require a lot of officials. In a goldfish bowl it tests your physical and mental skills, your patience, and your perseverance and you play in all kinds of conditions. You get lousy breaks, and good breaks, and you have to cope. It is almost life.
Deane Beman
The Times, 1 January 1987

16   Have you ever noticed what golf spells backwards?
Al Boliska
Laurence J. Peter, *Peter's Quotations,* 1977

17   If I am faced with a short putt in a crisis, I don't think how I am going to swing the putter or how I am going to strike the ball; my one aim is to will the ball into the hole.
Michael Bonallack
Donald Steel, *The Golfer's Bedside Book,* 1971

18   Good scoring golf involves – in addition to swinging the clubs correctly – analysis, judgment, planning and decisions.
Edward F. Chui
Golf, 1969, Ch. 9

19   Golf is a game whose aim is to hit a very small ball into an even smaller hole, with weapons singularly ill-designed for the purpose.
Sir Winston Churchill (1874–1965)
Attributed

20   It's better to have a twenty-foot uphill putt than a six-foot downhill one.
Russell Clayden
Sunday Times, 20 August 1989

21   During his downswing, a good golfer can generate up to four horse-power.
Alastair Cochran and John Stobbs
The Search for the Perfect Swing, 1968, Ch. 1

22   You've got to be hard with yourself, to be arrogant on the course. . . . You must never ever stop trying over every shot.
Neil Coles
Sunday Times, 23 May 1982

23   Golf . . . I came to regard as a holy exercise.
Alistair Cooke
Six Men, 1977, 'H. L. Mencken'

24   There's more tension in golf than in boxing because golfers bring it on themselves. It's silly really because it's not as if the golf ball is going to jump up and belt you on the whiskers, is it?
Henry Cooper
Norman Giller, *The Book of Golf Lists*, 1985

25   The charm of golf lies in the constant challenge it offers to every golfer, no matter whether he is a Tony Jacklin or the humblest of rabbits.
Geoffrey Cousins
The Handbook of Golf, 1969, Preface

26   Gentlemen play golf.
Bing Crosby
Bob Chieger and Pat Sullivan, *The Book of Golf Quotations*, 1987

27   I found a sponsor for my first year as a professional. But since then I have also found a wife, a child and a mortgage.
David Curry
Independent, 'Quotes of the Week', 25 March 1989

28   Golf is like a love affair: if you don't take it seriously, it's no fun; if you do take it seriously, it breaks your heart.
Arnold Daly
Laurence J. Peter, *Peter's Quotations*, 1977

29   It is not a crime to play a bad shot and the player may yet be a good husband and father and a true Christian gentleman.
Bernard Darwin
Attributed

30   If I could have turned the clock back, I'd have picked a career in golf instead.
Ted Dexter
Sunday Telegraph, 'Quotes 1989', 24 December 1989

31 I fully recognize how extraordinarily difficult it is to play golf to a professional level. I always thought that temperamentally I may not have been well suited to it. Cricket is kinder on the soul.
Ted Dexter
Independent, 5 January 1990

32 I prefer golf to tennis; all tennis courts look alike.
Brad Dillman
John Samuel, *The Guardian Book of Sports Quotes*, 1985

33 Real golfers go to work to relax.
George Dillon
Bob Chieger and Pat Sullivan, *The Book of Golf Quotations*, 1987

34 Golf is like the eighteen-year-old girl with the big boobs. You know it's wrong but you can't keep away from her.
Val Doonican
Independent, 'Quotes of the Week', 11 November 1989

35 Playing the game [golf], I have learned the meaning of humility. It has given me an understanding of the futility of human effort.
Abba Eban
Sunday Times, 10 July 1977

36 Nothing will be left to chance. You want to know the course so well that you know it by heart. In the end you want to go to sleep at night thinking about it.
Nick Faldo
Sunday Times, 12 July 1981

37 I'd trade everything I've done this year, all the good places, all the wins, all the money, just for one major.
Nick Faldo
Independent, 'Quotes of the Week', 5 November 1988

38 I didn't like team sports because it annoyed me that if you do your bit you could still go home a loser.
Nick Faldo
The Times, 11 April 1989

39 From being a kid it has been my dream to leave a legacy. I want people to say 'Did you see Nick Faldo play?'
Nick Faldo
Independent, 13 April 1989

40   To be the best in the world you've got to play around the world.

Nick Faldo
Independent, 7 October 1989

41   If you are two or three ahead, then it is all right to lose, but with a lead like that [eleven strokes] you've got nowhere to go because losing would make you a real prat.

David Feherty
Observer, 22 October 1989

42   The difference between a good golf shot and a bad one is the same as the difference between a beautiful and a plain woman – a matter of millimetres.

Ian Fleming (1908–64)
Goldfinger, 1959, Ch. 8

43   A golf club is the extension of one's home; the election of members is purely a domestic matter.

W. G. L. Folkard
Geoffrey Cousins, *Golf in Britain,* 1975, Ch. 26

44   He's had no birdies, relatively few pars, a number of bogies and a heckuva lot of double bogies.

Gerald R. Ford (on Jimmy Carter)
New York Times, 21 May 1978

45   I know I'm getting better at golf because I'm hitting fewer spectators.

Gerald R. Ford
Bob Chieger and Pat Sullivan, *The Book of Golf Quotations,* 1987

46   Golf always makes me so damned angry.

King George V (1865 – 1936)
Attributed

47   You get to know more of the character of a man in a round of golf than you can get to know in six months with only political experience.

David Lloyd George (1863–1945)
Observer, 'Sayings of the Week', 27 January 1924

48 Golf is the only game where the worst player gets the best of it. He obtains more out of it as regards both exercise and enjoyment, for the good player gets worried over the slightest mistake, whereas the poor player makes too many mistakes to worry over them.

David Lloyd George (1863–1945)
Bob Chieger and Pat Sullivan, *The Book of Golf Quotations*, 1987
(See also Milne *below)*

49 In golf, as in medicine . . . the best way to get out of trouble is to avoid it.

Richard Gordon
Dr Gordon's Casebook, 1982, '12 February'

50 The game ain't over till the fat lady sings.

David Graham
Sunday Times, 17 June 1984

51 If you watch a game it's fun. If you play it, it's recreation. If you work at it, it's golf.

Bob Hope
Attributed

52 Pinky Kerr is on th' decline but refuses t' consult a doctor fer fear he'll tell him t' play golf.

Frank McKinney Hubbard (1868–1930)
New Sayings By Abe Martin, 1917

53 You'd better be careful any time you play golf with President Johnson – he always brings his own Birdies.

Hubert H. Humphrey
Sports Illustrated, 26 August 1968

54 In golf you've got to keep down your emotions. You can't release the pressure. You have to eat it.

Tony Jacklin
Sunday Times, 6 June 1982

55 In some ways it takes more guts to quit than it does to carry on. Some people carry on playing tournaments because they have nothing else to do.

Tony Jacklin
The Times, 11 September 1985

56   Remember that golf is a game of how many, not how; that people may often be interested in *what* you scored, but rarely in *how*.

John Jacobs and Ken Bowden
Play Better Golf with John Jacobs, 1969, Ch. 13

57   The game is never over until the last putt has been holed.

John Jacobs and Ken Bowden
Ibid.

58   One reason . . . why golf can become such a difficult game is simply because there are so many different ways of playing it correctly; and that one secret, for any golfer striving to improve, is to decide first which way is his or her own correct way.

John Jacobs
Donald Steel, *The Golfer's Bedside Book*, 1971

59   Putting is seventy per cent technique, thirty per cent mental.

Mark James
Sunday Times, 13 September 1981

60   Whether I am playing for £1 or £41 000 makes no odds. I don't need any inspiration.

Mark James
Independent, 'Quotes of the Week', 11 March 1989

61   The devoted golfer is an anguished soul who has learned a lot about putting, just as an avalanche victim has learned a lot about snow.

Dan Jenkins
Sports Illustrated, 16 July 1962

62   With very few exceptions, the best golfers all the world over taught themselves.

J. C. Jessop
Teach Yourself Golf, 1950, Ch. 1

63   One reason golf is such an exasperating game is that a thing learned is so easily forgotten and we find ourselves struggling year after year with faults we had discovered and corrected time and again.

Bobby Jones
Donald Steel, *The Golfer's Bedside Book*, 1971

64   Walter Travis, probably the greatest putter the game has ever seen, always said that he visualized the putting stroke as an attempt to drive an imaginary tack into the back of the ball.
Bobby Jones
Ibid.

65   It is nothing new or original to say that golf is played one stroke at a time. But it took me many years to realize it.
Bobby Jones
John Stobbs, *At Random through the Green*

66   Professional golfers were not pampered when I was young. We were kept in our place and never allowed to get purse-proud. But the winners didn't forget the losers. There was a good deal of playing for the glory and sharing the spoils, or spending it in the good old-fashioned style.
Andrew Kirkaldy
Fifty Years of Golf: My Memories, 1921

67   The only way you can make a golf course difficult for today's professional is to have small, fast undulating greens.
Tom Kite
The Times, 7 August 1986

68   You can't see inside guys, into their minds, or their stomachs. I'm aggressive, but because there are lots of guys out there with real fast swings who hit the ball miles, they get called aggressive and I get called conservative. It just ain't so.
Tom Kite
Guardian, 21 March 1989

69   This is the twelfth–the green is like a plateau with the top shaved off.
Renton Laidlaw
Private Eye, No. 591, 10 August 1984

> 70   'I'm off my game,' the golfer said,
>   And shook his locks in woe;
>   'My putter never lays me dead,
>   My drives will never go;
>   Howe'er I swing, howe'er I stand,
>   Results are still the same,
>   I'm in the but, I'm in the sand–
>   I'm off my game!'
>   Andrew Lang (1844–1912)
>   *Off My Game*

71   I don't mind being the ex-Masters champion. It feels a lot better than not being an ex-Masters champion.
Sandy Lyle
The Times, 13 April 1989

72   It is almost impossible to remember how tragic a place the world is when one is playing golf.
Robert Lynd
Rudolf Flesch, *The Book of Unusual Quotations*, 1959

73   I kept hanging on to my clubs like I hang on to the steering wheel of one of my cars, and that is the worst possible thing I could do.
Nigel Mansell
Independent, 'Quotes of the Week', 26 November 1988

74   If you drink, don't drive. Don't even putt.
Dean Martin
B. Rowes, *The Book of Quotes*, 1979

75   If I had my way, any man guilty of golf would be ineligible for any office of trust under these United States.
H. L. Mencken (1880–1956)
Alistair Cooke, *Six Men*, 1977

76   Golf is so popular simply because it is the best game in the world at which to be bad . . . At golf it is the bad player who gets the most strokes.
A. A. Milne
Not That It Matters, 1919
(*See also* Lloyd George *above*)

77   The game of golf was not invented, it happened.
John Morgan
Golf, 1976, 'Introduction to the Game'

78   When properly played, golf is fun; it is also a mental and physical stimulus, a revitalizer of brain and body. But as played by ninety-nine out of a hundred people, it results in mental strain, nerve-racking and actual physical suffering.
Alex J. Morrison
A New Way to Better Golf, 1932, Ch. I

79   That's what you play for, to separate yourself from the crowd.
Jack Nicklaus
Sports Illustrated, 8 March 1971

80   Last week I made a double bogey and didn't even get mad.
Now that's bad.
Jack Nicklaus
New York Times, 24 July 1977

81   That's one nice thing about golf – it's a humbling game. Golf
is the only sport where, if you win twenty per cent of the time,
you're the best. In other sports you must win as much as ninety per
cent of the time to be the absolute best.
Jack Nicklaus
New York Times, 23 July 1978

82   In golf you're always breaking a barrier. When you bust it,
you set yourself a little higher barrier, and try to break that one.
Jack Nicklaus
Barbara Rowes, *The Book of Quotes*, 1979

83   Part of the game is getting poor lies and good lies and playing
the ball as it lies.
Jack Nicklaus
New York Times, 23 August 1980

84   I tee the ball high because years of experience have shown me
that air offers less resistance than dirt.
Jack Nicklaus
John Samuel, *The Guardian Book of Sports Quotes*, 1985

85   Sometimes I drive well, sometimes I pitch and chip well,
sometimes I putt well, but they don't always work together well.
Jack Nicklaus
The Times, 2 June 1986

86   I don't remember too much about the tournaments I lose.
Jack Nicklaus
New York Times, 12 April 1987

87   Augusta is the kind of course that eliminates two-thirds of the
guys before they tee-off. It has brought the cream to the top every
year so it shouldn't be too hard to keep on winning.
Jack Nicklaus
Sunday Times, 2 April 1989

88   I will stop only when I think I can no longer win.

Jack Nicklaus
Sunday Telegraph, 21 January 1990

89   Golf teaches you how to behave. A kid who plays golf is different from a lot of other athletes because he hasn't had his own way. He's had to get on with older people, and if he won't play by their rules he can't play at all.

Jack Nicklaus
Sunday Times, 21 January 1990

90   It doesn't bother me what ball I use, what colour trousers I wear or what I ate the night before. How can that sort of stuff have any effect on your game?

Greg Norman
Sunday Times, 23 September 1984

91   Oh well, no matter what happens I can always dig ditches for a living.

Arnold Palmer
Norman Giller, *The Book of Golf Lists,* 1985

92   Golf is merely an expensive way of leaving home.

Michael Parkinson
Bats in the Pavilion, 1977, Ch. 1

93   'Golf,' he replied, 'was much too serious a matter to be called a sport.'

John Pearson
James Bond: The Authorised Biography of 007, 1973, Ch. 2

94   It's good sportsmanship to not pick up lost golf balls while they are still rolling.

Laurence J. Peter
Peter's Quotations, 1977

95   God won't stop me entering the kingdom of heaven just because I play sport on Sunday.

Gary Player
Melbourne *Age,* 2 January 1982
Bill Wannan, *Great Aussie Quotes,* 1982

96   They say some men are good putters or good chippers. Nonsense, the whole secret of golf is to choose the right club for the shot.
Gary Player
John Samuel, *The Guardian Book of Sports Quotes*, 1985

97   If you think of yourself as an unlucky golfer, if you're sure you'll get a bad bounce, if you think you'll land in the water then you *will* be unlucky and get the bad bounce and land in the water.
Gary Player
Norman Giller, *The Book of Golf Lists*, 1985

98   Spectator: Lucky shot.
     Gary Player: You're right. The more I practise, the luckier I get.
Gary Player
The Times, 1 April 1989

99   You have to be aggressive, and that's the way I've been playing recently. I've been reading some articles about Arnold Palmer, and how he became so great. If they put a flag on the *Titanic*, Arnie would buy a scuba-diving outfit and go for it.
Juan 'Chi Chi' Rodriguez
New York Times, 5 July 1987

100   I'm playing like Tarzan – and scoring like Jane.
Juan 'Chi Chi' Rodriguez
Attributed

101   I guess there is nothing that will get your mind off everything like golf will. I have never been depressed enough to take up the game, but they say you can get so sore at yourself that you forget to hate your enemies.
Will Rogers
Bob Chieger and Pat Sullivan, *The Book of Golf Quotations*, 1987

102   [Golf is] just the old-fashioned pool hall moved outdoors, but with no chairs around the walls.
Will Rogers
Ibid.

103   I think those golfers who look as though they got dressed in the dark should be penalized two strokes each for offending the public eye.
Doug Sanders
Norman Giller, *The Book of Golf Lists*, 1985

104 Actors and actresses are so busy trying to be ladies and gentlemen and golfers that they have no time left to pay attention to their jobs.
Osbert Sitwell (1892–1969)
Observer, 'Sayings of the Week', 5 September 1926

105 A golf course outside a big town serves an excellent purpose in that it segregates, as though in a concentration camp, all the idle and idiot well-to-do.
Osbert Sitwell
Attributed

106 Hard by [Leith] in the fields called the Links, the citizens of Edinburgh divert themselves at a game called golf, in which they use a curious kind of bats, tipt with horn, and small elastic balls of leather, stuffed with feathers, rather less than tennis balls, but of a much harder consistence. This they strike with such force and dexterity from one hole to another, that they will fly to an incredible distance.
Tobias Smollett (1721–71)
The Expedition of Humphry Clinker, 1771, Vol. II

107 I was shewn one particular set of golfers, the youngest of whom was turned fourscore. They were all gentlemen of independent fortunes, who had amused themselves with this pastime for the best part of a century, without having ever felt the least alarm from sickness or disgust; and they never went to bed, without having each the best part of a gallon of claret in his belly.
Tobias Smollet (1721–71)
Ibid.

108 If a lot of people gripped a knife and fork like they do a golf club, they'd starve to death.
Sam Snead
Sports Illustrated, 8 August 1966

109 My first club was a swamp maple I cut and used to knock acorns.
Sam Snead
Donald Steel, *The Golfer's Bedside Book*, 1971

110 You have to stand in the right way and grip the club in the right way, and then simply swing.
J. L. Stobbs (to his son, John, aged eight)
John Stobbs, *Tackle Golf This Way*, 1961

111   Apply yourself to the ball – and the ball will do the rest.
John Stobbs
Ibid., Ch. 12

112   It's funny that everybody who used to call Curtis Strange the hothead who was so hard on himself are now calling him a great competitor. What's the difference?
Curtis Strange
New York Times, 13 June 1988

113   Golf is a lovely relaxer on cricket tours.
E. W. Swanton
Swanton in Australia with MCC 1946–1975, 1975, Ch. 6

114   I'm a very bad player. My golf gets worse and worse. I just don't have the time, although to read some of you newspaper chappies people would think I spent my life on the course.
Denis Thatcher
Independent, 11 February 1989

115   For four years through the war I hacked away and slowly got the hang of it. During that time there was nobody to instruct me or put me wrong and I found that, by the end of the war, I had a single figure handicap and, fortunately, was on the right track.
Peter Thomson
Donald Steel, *The Golfer's Bedside Book*, 1971

116   Boredom is the curse of the intelligent man. It destroys interest, incentive, concentration and eventually application. It wrecks a golfer.
Peter Thomson
Sunday Times, 29 May 1983

117   Golf needs a wind just as much as sailing.
Peter Thomson
The Times, 18 July 1984

118   I'm hitting the driver so good, I gotta dial the operator for long distance after I hit it.
Lee Trevino
New York Times, 21 May 1978

119   Some may hit the ball for miles but they are not winners, they just lose their ball.
Lee Trevino
The Times, 9 August 1978

120   My whole game revolves around one club, the putter.
Lee Trevino
Ibid.

121   I've avoided playing thirty-six holes in one day in a tournament for more than five years. The only time I would usually consider playing more than eighteen is when my wife Claudia insists that I give her a lesson.
Lee Trevino
The Times, 23 June 1984

122   Golf is good walk spoiled.
Mark Twain (1835–1910)
Attributed

123   No matter what happens, keep on hitting the ball.
Harry Vardon
Donald Steel, *The Golfer's Bedside Book*, 1971

124   [Seve Ballesteros] doesn't hit the ball, he strokes it.
Paul Way
Sunday Times, 23 September 1984

125   Since I first watched the game on television when I was ten I have been motivated by the thought of winning the Open [Championship at Muirfield].
Ian Woosnam
The Times, 16 July 1987

126   Every hole is a good test of golf.
Ian Woosnam
Guardian, 28 October 1989

127   Maybe I should read my own book. I am not that happy with my game.
Ian Woosnam (author of *Power Golf*)
Sunday Telegraph, 'Quotes 1989', 24 December 1989

128   I don't just want to be remembered as a good golfer, I also want people to think of me as a nice guy.
Fuzzy Zoeller
The Times, 20 June 1984

129   Nothing rolls like a ball.
Fuzzy Zoeller
Ibid.

130   Without the people, I'd be playing in front of trees for a couple of hundred dollars.
Fuzzy Zoeller
Sports Illustrated, 6 August 1984

41   GREYHOUND RACING

See also 19 Coursing

1   It is natural for a grey-hound to have a long tail.
Thomas Fuller (1654–1734)
Gnomologia, 1732, No. 2983

2   My grandfather couldn't prescribe a pill to make a greyhound run faster, but he could produce one to make the other five go slower.
Benny Green
John Samuel, *The Guardian Book of Sports Quotes*, 1985

3   I do not know how many noble Lords have gone to the dogs.
Lord Newell (on greyhound racing)
House of Lords, 15 January 1985

4   I see you stand like greyhounds in the slips,
Straining upon the start.
William Shakespeare (1564–1616)
Henry V, 1598–99, Act III, Sc. I

5   Edward and Richard, like a brace of greyhounds
Having the fearful flying hare in sight.
William Shakespeare (1564–1616)
Henry VI Pt. III 1590–91, Act II, Sc. V

6	*Slender:*	How does your fallow greyhound, sir? I heard say he was outrun on Cotsale.
	Page:	It could not be judged, sir.
	Slender:	You'll not confess; you'll not confess.
	Shallow:	That he will not; – 'tis your fault; 'tis your fault: – 'Tis a good dog.
	Page:	A cur, sir.
	Shallow:	Sir, he's a good dog, and a fair dog. Can there more be said? he is good and fair.

William Shakespeare (1564–1616)
Merry Wives of Windsor, 1597–1601, Act I, Sc. I

7 Although I cannot keep a grey-hound, may not a grey-hound help to keep me?
Jonathan Swift (1667–1745)
A Letter to the King at Arms

8 Greyhound racing is a mechanized version of coursing for the industrial age and the mass society, without the skill and variety of the field sport – and without the blistering pace.
Geoffrey Wheatcroft
Sunday Telegraph, 1 March 1987

42 GYMNASTICS

1 Gymnastics open the chest, exercise the limbs, and give a man all the pleasure of boxing without the blows. I could wish that learned men would lay out the time they employ in controversies and disputes about nothing, in this method of fighting with their own shadows. It might conduce very much to evaporate the spleen, which makes them uneasy to the public as well as to themselves.
Joseph Addison (1672–1719)
Tryon Edwards, *The New Dictionary of Thoughts*

2 The most important aspect of gymnastics is to show what the human body is capable of.
Leonid Arkaev
The Times, 18 October 1989

3 I come to the gym regularly, even before my deadline.
[Gymnastics] relieves tension – it's much better than valium.
Susan Reed
New York Times, 19 June 1978

43 HANDBALL

1 [Handball] is one of the few games that can be played with
enjoyment almost from the first time one steps on the court.
John H. Shaw
Handball, 1971, 'Concept' I

2 The most ancient amusement of this kind [ball games], is
distinguished with us by the name of hand-ball, and is, if Homer
may be accredited, coeval at least with the destruction of Troy.
Joseph Strutt (1749–1802)
The Sports and Pastimes of the People of England, 1801, Bk. II, Ch. III, I

44 HANG GLIDING
See also 39 Gliding

1 Hang gliding is a vital, exciting facet of the general aviation
scene and represents a credit to the innovative and adventurous
spirit so long absent from non-commercial flying.
David Esler
Dan Poynter, *Hang Gliding*, 1977

2 The most dangerous part of hang gliding is the male ego.
Donnita Holland
Ibid.

3 It's such a direct form of flying. There are no sticks or
controls; you move your body weight, that's all . . . And there's no
fuselage, nothing between you and the ground. You just feel free.
Judy Leden
Independent, 13 May 1989

4   Every hang glider is jealous of birds. When we're not flying we're watching them. Marvellous creatures – leave us for dead.
Graham Slater
Sunday Times, 25 October 1981

5   The air! Man has visions of flight – not the roaring progress of heavy sinking machines, but that silent loveliness of gliding on outstretched arms that comes to everyone in dreams.
Frank S. Stuart
City of the Bees, quoted in Dan Poynter, *Hang Gliding*, 1977

---

45   HARNESS RACING

See also 16 Chariot Racing

---

1   Harness racing is the nearest thing to chariot racing to be seen today.
Veronica Heath
The Times, 22 October 1988

---

46   HAWKING

---

1   Hawking is a pleasure for high mounting spirits; such as will not stoope to inferiour lures, having their mindes so farre above, as they scorne to partake of them.
Richard Braithwaite (1588?–1673)
The English Gentleman, 1630

2   Hawking comes near to hunting, the one in the air, as the other on the earth, a sport as much affected as the other, by some preferred.
Robert Burton (1577–1640)
The Anatomy of Melancholy, Pt. II, Sec. II

3   He has been out a hawking for butterflies.
Thomas Fuller (1654–1734)
Gnomologia, 1732, No. 1863

4   High-flying hawks are fit for princes.
Thomas Fuller (1654–1734)
Ibid., No. 2500

5   Hold fast is the first point in hawking.
Thomas Fuller (1654–1734)
Ibid., No. 2520

6   I suppose the civil wars put an end to hawking; the old establishments were broken up; and it never seems to have been in fashion afterwards.
Robert Southey (1774–1843)
Southey's Common Place Book, First Series

47   HOCKEY (FIELD)

See also 48 Hockey (Ice)

1   All you need to keep goal is a lot of courage, lightning reflexes, and more intelligence than anyone else in the team.
Wendy Banks
The Times, 24 September 1988

2   A good goalkeeper makes the job look easy.
Carol A. Bryant
Hockey for Schools, 1969, Ch. 4

3   So many sporting activities have nowadays become businesses, but hockey is, and I hope always will be, a leisure-time entertainment.
Vera Chapman
Tackle Hockey This Way, 1961, Introduction

4   We badly need more synthetic surfaces because the run of the ball is more reliable on them and they give greater rein to players' skills. That will increase our chances of drawing larger crowds and, therefore, TV since games will be faster, breakdowns in play will be fewer and more action will result. Right now, the average club game here is even more boring than your average Football League match, and that's saying something.

Richard Dodds
Financial Times, 6 August 1988

5   We are in tune with the times because it [hockey] is a game where you can be a complete individual while remaining very much part of a team effort.

Hockey Association
Sunday Times, 20 November 1988

6   When I first came into the game, it was far more casual, virtually a case of turning up and introducing yourself in the changing room. Now we have fitness schedules, training weekends and tournaments virtually all the year round. It is getting increasingly difficult to hold down a well-paid job and play top-class hockey.

Richard Leman
Sunday Correspondent, 12 November 1989

7   Women's hockey has changed ... The traditional type of hockey player – you know, enormous, burly – just doesn't exist any more. We're not like the old type of hockey player at all. We are athletes. You need a slim, light build to play hockey these days.

Alison Ramsey
The Times, 24 September 1988

8   To many players the position of goalkeeper is the least to be desired of any, mainly perhaps because they strongly object to standing between a couple of posts to be shot at.

S. H. Shoveller
Hockey, 1922, Ch. XVIII

9   Great Britain have turned upside down the pages of world hockey history.

Nigel Starmer-Smith
Private Eye, No. 593, 7 September 1984

10   We need to lose our middle-class image. I'd like to see kids playing this game in the streets of cities like Liverpool.
Ian Taylor
The Times, 1 January 1987

48   HOCKEY (ICE)

See also 47 Hockey (Field)

1   Home ice means something if you win your home games.
Al Arbour
New York Times, 1 May 1979

2   I've never sent a player out to get another player. But to break his concentration, that's another thing, eh?
Scotty Bowman
New York Times, 17 May 1979

3   A hungry player is the best player, and the hungry coach is the best coach.
Don Cherry
New York Times, 16 May 1978

4   I went to a fight last night and an ice hockey game broke out.
Rodney Dangerfield
Sports Illustrated, 4 September 1978

5   I'm lucky. I'm God-gifted, and I'm the first one to admit it.
Wayne Gretzy
Sunday Correspondent, 17 December 1989

6   Nobody in the world can go hard for two minutes. A minute and a half is max.
Leo Koopmans
Guardian, 7 October 1989

7   I like controlling the puck, getting the guys to run after me. It's like you're laughing at the other guys. You've got the puck. 'Come and get it!'
Guy Lafleur
New York Times, 15 May 1978

8   We [goalkeepers] can be compared to a pitcher in baseball, but at least he holds the ball, and in that way can control the team's destiny. All we can do is watch, wait and react.

Mike Luit
New York Times, 5 May 1986

9   Hockey is a game of mistakes.

Frank Mahovlich
Ice Hockey, 1964, Ch. 10

10   Most of the teams we [Britain] play against have either a Canadian or Eastern Bloc method. We're in between. We don't have any method really.

Terry Matthews
Guardian, 21 March 1989

11   You take the man, you don't fake him.

Mike Nykoluk
New York Times, 7 May 1979

12   I sleep well the night before a game and I try to dream about what is going to happen in the game – where they drop the puck, if they shoot.

Patrick Roy
New York Times, 5 May 1986

13   Why push and shove? All you have to do is nudge someone at the last second.

Fred Shero
New York Times, 17 May 1979

14   Continentals don't like it up 'em.

Paul Smith
Independent, 'Quotes of the Week', 25 March 1989

15   Canada is a country whose main exports are hockey players and cold fronts. Our main imports are baseball players and acid rain.

Pierre Trudeau
Sports Illustrated, 26 July 1982

49 HUNTING

1 That *Caput lupinum* that *hostis humani generis,* as an honourable friend of mine once called him in his place, that *fera naturae*–a poacher.
Henry Peter Brougham (1778–1868)
House of Commons, 7 February 1828

2 If you are involved in any kind of hunting operation on a sensible scale, the hunter is the only person who wants that species to survive.
Duke of Edinburgh
Observer, 'Sayings of the Week', 10 January 1984

3 Hunting has as much pain as pleasure.
Thomas Fuller (1654–1734)
Gnomologia, 1732, No. 2576

4 It is a good hunting-bout, that fills the belly.
Thomas Fuller (1654–1734)
Ibid., No. 2856

> 5 By hawk and by hound,
> Small profit is found
> Thomas Fuller (1654–1734)
> *Ibid.,* 1732, No. 6339

> 6 If once we efface the joys of the chase
> From the land and outroot the Stud,
> Goodbye to the Anglo-Saxon race!
> Farewell to the Norman blood.
> Adam Lindsay Gordon (1833–70)
> *Wearie Wayfarer,* 7

7 What a cheerful sound is that of the hunters, issuing from the autumnal wood and sweeping over the hill and dale!
> –'A cry more tuneable
> Was never halloo'd to by hound or horn.'
What sparkling richness in the scarlet coats of the riders, what a glittering confusion in the pack, what spirit in the horses, what eagerness in the followers on foot, as they disperse over the plain, or force their way over hedge and ditch!
William Hazlitt (1778–1830)
Merry England

8   The English are the only nation who ride hard a-hunting.
Samuel Johnson (1709–84)
Boswell's *Life of Johnson*, 24 September 1773

9   It is very strange and very melancholy that the paucity of human pleasures should persuade us ever to call hunting one of them.
Samuel Johnson (1709–84)
Mrs Piozzi's *Anecdotes*, 1786

10   A houndless hunter, and a gunless gunner see ay game enough.
James Kelly
Scottish Proverbs, 1721, A, No. 164

11   A keeper is only a poacher turned outside in, and a poacher is a keeper turned inside out.
Charles Kingsley (1819–75)
The Water Babies, 1863, Ch. 1

> 12   Hunting is the hero's joy,
>   Till war his nobler game supplies.
>   Thomas Moore (1779–1852)
>   *Hilli-Ho!*

13   Often hounds stray in vain through the mountain glens and a stag, almost by accident, falls into the nets.
Ovid (43 BC–AD 17)
The Art of Love, III

14   Good and much company, and a good dinner; most of their discourse was about hunting, in a dialect I understand very little.
Samuel Pepys (1633–1703)
Diary, 22 November 1663

> 15   Waken, lords and ladies gay
>   On the mountain dawns the day,
>   All the jolly chase is here,
>   With hawk, and horse, and hunting spear;
>   Hounds are in their couples yelling,
>   Hawks are whistling, horns are knelling,
>   Merrily, merrily, mingle they,
>   'Waken, lords and ladies gay'.
>   Sir Walter Scott (1771–1832)
>   *Hunting Song*

16   Huntsman, rest! thy chase is done.
Sir Walter Scott (1771–1832)
Lady of the Lake, 1810, Canto I, St. 32

17   Come, shall we go an kill us venison?
And yet it irks me, the poor dappled fools,
Being native burghers of this desert city,
Should, in their own confines, with forked heads
Have their round haunches gor'd.
William Shakespeare (1564–1616)
As You Like It, 1596–1600, Act II, Sc. I

18   This is not hunters' language.–He that strikes
The venison first shall be the lord o' the feast.
William Shakespeare (1564–1616)
Cymbeline, 1609–10, Act III, Sc. III

19   Moody mad and desperate stags
Turn on the bloody hounds with heads of steel.
William Shakespeare (1564–1616)
Henry VI Pt. I, 1589–90, Act IV, Sc. II

20   Hold, Warwick, seek thee out some other chase,
For I myself must hunt this deer to the death.
William Shakespeare (1564–1616)
Henry VI Pt. II, 1590–91, Act V, Sc. II

21   Hunting was his daily exercise.
William Shakespeare (1564–1616)
Henry VI Pt. III, 1590–91, Act IV, Sc. VI

22   The king he is hunting the deer; I am coursing myself.
William Shakespeare (1564–1616)
Love's Labour's Lost, 1594–95, Act IV, Sc. III

23   I do follow here in the chase, not like a hound that hunts, but one that fills up the cry.
William Shakespeare (1564–1616)
Othello, 1604–5, Act II, Sc. III

24   Huntsman, I charge thee, tender well my hounds.
William Shakespeare (1564–1616)
The Taming of the Shrew, 1593–94, Induction, Sc. I

25   'Tis well, sir, that you hunted for yourself;
     'Tis thought your deer does hold you at a bay.
William Shakespeare (1564–1616)
Ibid., Act V, Sc. II

26   To-morrow, an it please your majesty
     To hunt the panther and the hart with me,
     With horn and hound we'll give your grace bonjour.
William Shakespeare (1564–1616)
Titus Andronicus, 1593–94, Act I, Sc. I

27   The hunt is up, the morn is bright and gay,
     The fields are fragrant, and the woods are green,
     Uncouple here, and let us make a bay,
     And wake the emperor and his lovely bride,
     And rouse the prince, and ring a hunter's peal,
     That all the court may echo with the noise.
William Shakespeare (1564–1616)
Ibid.

28   She hearkens for his hounds, and for his horn:
       Anon she hears them chant it lustily,
       And all in haste she coasteth to the cry.
William Shakespeare (1564–1616)
Venus and Adonis, 1592

29   For now she knows it is no gentle chase,
     But the blunt boar, rough bear or lion proud,
     Because the cry remaineth in one place,
     Where fearfully the dogs exclaim aloud:
       Finding their enemy to be so curst,
       They all strain court'sy who shall cope him first.
William Shakespeare (1564–1616)
Ibid.

30   Would any but these boiled brains of nineteen and
two-and-twenty hunt in this weather?
William Shakespeare (1564–1616)
The Winter's Tale, 1610–11, Act III, Sc. III

31   It isn't mere convention. Everyone can see that the people
who hunt are the right people, and the people who don't are the
wrong ones.
George Bernard Shaw (1856–1950)
Heartbreak House, 1919, Act III

32   The law may multiply penalties by reams. Squires may fret and justices commit, and gamekeepers and poachers continue their nocturnal wars. There must be game on Lord Mayor's day, do what you will. You may multiply the crimes by which it is procured; but nothing can arrest its inevitable progress from the wood of the esquire to the spit of the citizen.

Sydney Smith (1771–1845)
Game Laws

> 33   Invites thee to the chase, the sport of kings;
> Image of war, without its guilt.
>
> William Somerville (1675–1742)
> *The Chase,* 1735

34   Hunting has now an idea of quality joined to it, and is become the most important business in the life of a gentleman. Anciently it was quite otherwise. M. Fleury has severely remarked that this extravagant passion for hunting is a strong proof of our Gothic extraction, and shows an affinity of humour with the savage Americans.

William Walsh (1663–1708)
Preface to Dryden, *The Pastorals,* 1697

35   Hunting is ninety per cent of the fun of war for ten per cent of the risk.

Philip Warbuton Lee
Independent, 2 October 1989

---

50   HURDLES

---

1   [Hurdles] . . . the mankiller of track and field.

Anonymous

2   A good high hurdler must have a leg that is one metre long, have the speed of a sprinter, be technically sound, have the strength of a 400-metre man, and the courage of a tiger.

Guy Drut
Wilbur L. Ross, *The Hurdler's Bible,* 3rd ed., 1978

3   The main thing is to get over the hurdles as quickly as possible, so you can do your fast running between them.

Roger Kingdom
The Times, 24 September 1988

4   I used to let the hurdles take advantage of me. Now I take advantage of them. If they get in the way, I try to break them.

Roger Kingdom
Sunday Telegraph, 12 March 1989

5   Losing makes it more exciting for the fans. They don't have me winning all the time; a little more suspense is good for the sport.

Edwin Moses
New York Times, 28 June 1987

6   Hurdles combine a sprinter, broad jumper, high jumper, and endurance of a 220 man!

Don F. Shy
Wilbur L. Ross, *The Hurdler's Bible*, 3rd ed., 1978

51   INJURIES

1   He's got to go in for a hernia operation, but when he gets over that he'll be back in harness again.

Peter Allis
Private Eye, No. 697, 2 September 1988

2   It's a tired athlete who gets injured.

Dr Ken Kingsbury
Independent, 'Quotes of the Week', 5 August 1989

52 JAVELIN

1   It's always the bad throws that hurt. On the good one, you can't feel a thing. It's similar to jumping off a wall: land perfectly and you don't feel it, land badly and you jar ankles and knees.

Steve Backley
Observer, 7 January 1990

2   I'm probably the weakest javelin thrower in the world, but I'm the fastest. . . . To me, it seems common sense that strong men are slow men.

Mike Hill
The Times, 2 July 1987

3   She's dragged the javelin back into the twentieth century.

Ron Pickering
John Samuel, *The Guardian Book of Sports Quotes*, 1985

4   If heaven had granted you the great bodily strength of a Nicostratus, I should object to your strong arms, made for combat in the arena, to be wasted on the tame sport of throwing the javelin or discus.

Tacitus (AD c. 55-c. 120)
Dialogue on Oratory, X

53 JOGGING

See also 58 Marathon
80 Running

1   My doc recently told me that jogging would add ten years to my life. He was right, I feel ten years older.

Milton Berle
John Samuel, *The Guardian Book of Sports Quotes*, 1985

2   I call it running because I do it for pleasure. Jogging implies an addiction.

Gedis Grudzinskas
Sunday Times Magazine, 30 November 1986

3   You may be jogging whiles your boots are green.
William Shakespeare (1564–1616)
The Taming of the Shrew, 1593–94, Act III, Sc. II

54   JUDO

1   I either go out and blast through everyone or it is spade work all the way.
Neal Adams
The Times, 28 September 1985

2   To win at judo you have to train, and with the right partners as well.
Neal Adams
Independent, 17 October 1989

3   I am twenty-six, and that is getting on for this kind of thing [major international competition in judo].
Stephen Gawthorpe
The Times, 7 August 1984

4   Judo skill is something like Pandora's box, only in this case whoever prises open the lid can gain all kinds of rich rewards.
G. R. Gleeson
Better Judo, 1972, Pt. 1

5   It's not like boxing. You can't work out your aggression by hitting. It's all so much a mental thing, you've got to make the other person *curl up* more. You see, judo is not just strength. It's *everything*.
Elvis Gordon
The Times, 24 September 1988

6   Even in judo, a good big man will generally beat a good little man.
Ray Stevens
Sunday Correspondent, 28 January 1990

55 KARATE

1 The trouble is, people don't take karate seriously as a competitive sport. They think we go round chopping trees down with our bare hands.

Ticky Donovan
Financial Times, 27 February 1988

2 Karate is like Christianity. Its history has been so riven by disputes between rival sects that sometimes the object of the devotion has been obscured.

Benjamin Raphael
John Samuel, *The Guardian Book of Sports Quotes,* 1985

56 KITE FLYING

1 Kite flying is as exciting as sex – and Mary Whitehouse can't ban it.

John Bally
John Samuel, *The Guardian Book of Sports Quotes,* 1985

2 The kite is a wonderful way of blowing away the cobwebs.

Ben Woodleigh
The Times, 25 February 1989

57 LACROSSE

1 Lacrosse, a game which requires the same qualities of combination, obedience, courage, individual unselfishness for the sake of the side – a player who attempts to keep the ball instead of passing it being absolutely useless – and is full of interest on account of the various kinds of skill required, fleetness of foot, quickness of eye, strength of wrist, and a great deal of judgment and knack. The game of lacrosse well played is a beautiful sight, the actions of the players being so full of grace and agility. The skill required, moreover, is so great that the attempt to acquire it is a splendid training in courage and perseverance. Here is a splendid field for the development of powers for organization, of good temper under trying circumstances, courage and determination to play up and do your best even in a losing game, rapidity of thought and action, judgment and self-reliance, and above all things, unselfishness and a knowledge of corporate action, learning to sink individual preferences in the effort of loyally working with others for the common good.

Dame Frances Dove
Margaret Boyd, *Lacrosse: Playing and Coaching,* 1959

2 [At Windsor Castle] I watched a game of la crosse played by a team of fourteeen Canadians and thirteen Iroquois Indians . . . The game was very pretty to watch . . . It is played with a ball and there is much running.

Queen Victoria (1819–1901)
Diary, 26 June 1876

58 MARATHON

1 The marathon is everyman's Everest.

Anonymous

2 Marathon running, the most punishing event in the world's sports calendar, is all in the mind.

Christopher Brasher
Observer, 20 October 1985

3   I am still looking for shoes that will make running on streets seem like running barefoot across the bosoms of maidens.

Dave Bronson
John Samuel, *The Guardian Book of Sports Quotes*, 1985

4   In a marathon you have to be very patient.

Julie Brown
New York Times, 25 June 1983

5   [Marathon running] is about determination and commitment and belief and why only when all three are complete and total, can you produce the performance which will give you that deep satisfaction, contentment and happiness beyond anything else I know.

Rob de Castella
Observer, 20 October 1985

6   I really didn't have a pre-race strategy. I do have a post-race strategy, and it involves me and some friends and a couple of beers.

Jerry Kiernan (after winning the New Jersey Waterfront Marathon)
New York Times, 27 April 1987

7   Running a marathon is just like reading a good book. After a while you're just not conscious of the physical act of reading.

Frank Shorter
Jonathon Green, *A Dictionary of Contemporary Quotations*, 1982

8   You do not run twenty-six miles on good looks and vitamin pills.

Frank Shorter
Brian Mitchell, *Running to Keep Fit*, 1984

9   Marathons get harder the more you do.

Ian Thompson
Guardian, 21 April 1989

10   You have to plan three years in advance. You are not running for today.

Douglas Wakiihuri
Guardian, 20 April 1989

11   Preparation for the marathon must all be as one. You need to run, to recover, to eat, to have shoes. You need all this, and so preparation for the race must become your life. Sometimes you run concentrating hard; and sometimes you can run relaxed, with a dead brain.

Douglas Wakiihuri
Sunday Times, 4 February 1990

59   MODERN PENTATHLON

1   To get to the top, you're bound to make a complete fool of yourself at some point in five events. It makes for a better atmosphere than most sports.

Sarah Parker
Sunday Times, 16 August 1981

2   You've got to be slightly mad to do pentathlon.

Sarah Parker
Ibid.

3   You can never get bored like I did with swimming. Its fascination is that each sport needs a totally different approach, and there's so much that can go wrong.

Kathy Taylor
Sunday Times, 16 August 1981

60   MOTOR CYCLING

1   You have to be able to throw the bike around like a BMX to get the right line for the next obstacle and often you experience the same frustration as golfers. Just when you're pleased with one drive up the fairway, you relax and make a mess of the next. In trials riding that's called falling off.

Robert Crawford
Observer, 12 March 1989

2   The bike is fine. I am the problem.
Eddie Lawson
Guardian, 25 March 1989

3   It's as hard as it looks. To try to have fun and ride your ass off is difficult.
Wayne Rainey
Observer, 6 August 1989

4   Every time you go out on a track you know you could die. I don't think about it, but I don't go faster than I have to. It's a business. I'm not in it for the glory, but I would like to retire a winner.
Kenny Roberts
Sunday Times, 31 July 1983

5   Motor-cycle racing is not a team sport.
Freddie Spencer
Sunday Times, 7 August 1983

6   Sometimes I take that extra risk. You have to to win races.
Kevin Swantz
Sunday Times, 6 August 1989

61   MOTOR RACING

See also 28 Drag Racing
60 Motor Cycling
62 Motor Rallying
92 Stock Car Racing

1   It doesn't take brute force. After all, I don't have to carry the car round on my shoulders. But it does take muscle. Neck muscles, wrist muscles.
Mario Andretti
Sunday Times, 10 July 1977

2   In motor racing there is no substitute for horsepower.
Anonymous

3   You don't have the right when you are a great driver to have a stupid accident which destroys the sporting spectacle.

Jean-Marie Balestre
Guardian, 1 November 1989

4   I don't believe in blindly following what everyone else does just because it proves to be successful on one car. There's too much 'copy, copy, copy' in this business . . . Just look at the latest crop of cars; they all look the same.

John Barnard
Independent, 23 March 1989

5   You may find this difficult to believe, but winning isn't as easy as it looks.

Ron Dennis
Independent, 9 July 1988

6   When the flag drops, the bullshit stops.

Frank Gardner
Attributed

7   Driving a racing car is like painting a picture. Anyone can doodle with a pencil. There are plenty of people who can turn out a reasonably recognizable sketch. But the real artists are few and far between. They are born, not made. Driving a racing car is just as much an art, it is not a knack that can be acquired. Either you have it or you have not.

Mike Hawthorn
Jonathon Green, *A Dictionary of Contemporary Quotations,* 1982

8   The first time you look at a race car, you have either a good feeling or a bad feeling. I had a very good feeling.

Howdy Holmes
New York Times, 17 May 1979

9   You appreciate that it is very easy to die and you have to arrange your life to cope with that reality.

Niki Lauda
Observer, 3 October 1982

10   The principle is the same, one man is champion, the others aren't.

Niki Lauda
Sunday Times, 19 August 1984

11   Danger is part of the game but not part of the appeal . . . The narrow margin of safety is not the buzz. The fact that you can smash your body to pieces by driving at 150 miles an hour is not the reason you do it.

Allan McNish
Observer, 22 October 1989

12   I don't mind having an accident when I can see it coming.

Nigel Mansell
Sunday Telegraph, 23 September 1989

13   It's necessary to relax your muscles when you can. Relaxing your brain is fatal.

Stirling Moss
James Beasley Simpson, *Best Quotes of '54, '55, '56*, 1957

14   One cannot really enjoy speed to the absolute limit if there's a destination involved.

Stirling Moss
Jonathon Green, *A Dictionary of Contemporary Quotations*, 1982

15   My only problem was maintaining concentration. After a few laps I had a fifteen-second lead, so I slowed down in order to save the tyres and gear box.

Nelson Piquet
New York Times, 31 March 1980

16   There's nothing natural about Formula One–I can't stand the artificiality.

Alain Prost
Sunday Times, 22 July 1984

17   When you start off as a driver, it is a sport; but when you get into Formula One, it suddenly becomes a job.

Alain Prost
Sunday Telegraph, 18 June 1989

18   Ayrton [Senna] has never accepted he could be overtaken, that's his big problem.

Alain Prost
Independent, 3 November 1989

19 Ayrton [Senna] has a small problem—he thinks he can't kill himself because he believes in God.

Alain Prost
Guardian, 4 November 1989

20 To be successful in racing . . . you need a double motivation; the skills of driving and the skills of organizing and finance.

Ayrton Senna
Sunday Times, 5 July 1987

21 There is no magic in Formula One, people can only go a bit faster than you around the corners.

Ayrton Senna
Sunday Times, 24 September 1989

22 It is all down to the fine tuning, the fine tuning of my car, its chassis and balance, and my body, my heart and my brain. To be at my peak I need to have them all together at their peaks at the same time. For me it is a task and a challenge every time I drive.

Ayrton Senna
Sunday Telegraph, 22 October 1989

23 The most important thing for me is to win. The few seconds of pleasure I get when I overtake, or gain a pole position, or win a race are my motivation.

Ayrton Senna
Sunday Correspondent, 5 November 1989

24 I wouldn't like to be sitting in Alain Prost's shoes right now.

Barry Sheen
Private Eye, No. 730, 8 December 1989

25 In my sport the quick are too often listed among the dead.

Jackie Stewart
Jonathon Green, *A Dictionary of Contemporary Quotations*, 1982

26 The talent required to drive a machine to the ultimate of its ability is the same, the same inherent chemical element is present today as when the sport began. Machines exist to be interpreted and understood.

Jackie Stewart
Sunday Times, 21 August 1983

27   Nelson Piquet must be furious with himself inside his helmet.
Murray Walker
Private Eye, No. 649, 31 October 1986

28   He's really got green fingers in engineering terms.
Murray Walker
Sunday Times, 9 August 1987

29   So, with half the race gone there's half the race to go!
Murray Walker
Private Eye, No. 670, 21 August 1987

30   Nigel Mansell–the Man of the Race; the Man of the Day; the Man from the Isle of Man.
Murray Walker
Independent, 'Quotes of the Week', 19 August 1989

31   [Motor racing is] an artistic form of bear baiting, in which the beast has to be teased and coaxed and teased some more, but never so much that it can bite back, because it bites back bad.
John Watson
Sunday Times, 19 July 1981

32   A racing driver is an artist, and driving is an expression of myself. It's not a job, but a definition of who I am.
John Watson
Sunday Times, 2 August 1981

62   MOTOR RALLYING

See also 60 Motor Cycling
61 Motor Racing
92 Stock Car Racing

1   It's the noise of the stones hitting the car, the knowledge I'm on the edge, that's so thrilling.
David Llewellin
Sunday Telegraph, 19 November 1989

2 You've got to be brave in this game. You've got to go for it. If we run out of road somewhere because of that, so be it . . .
David Llewellin
Ibid.

63 MOUNTAINEERING

1 Rivalry in mountaineering involves finding the quickest way up and the second quickest way down.
Anonymous

2 Great things are done when men and mountains meet;
This is not done by jostling in the street.
William Blake (1757–1827)
Great Things are Done

3 He that never climbed never fell.
John Heywood (1506–1565)
Proverbs, 1546, Pt. I, Ch. II

4 Because it is there.
George Mallory (in answer to the question why he wanted to climb Mount Everest, and reported in the *New York Times*, 18 March 1923. However some doubt has been cast on whether Mallory actually said these words. See Tom Holzel and Audrey Salkeld, *The Mystery of Mallory and Irving*, 1986. Mallory disappeared on Everest in 1924)

5 These athletes are terrible boasters. They climb the alps to crow.
George Meredith (1828–1909)
The Egoist, 1879

6 All mountains appear doomed to pass through the three stages: an inaccessible peak – the most difficult ascent in the Alps – an easy day for a lady.
A. F. Mummery
Attributed, 1893

7 The only thing on the level is mountain climbing.
Eddie Quinn
Laurence J. Peter, *Peter's Quotations*, 1977

64 NETBALL

See also 8 Basketball

---

1   I didn't like netball . . . I used to get wolf whistles because of my short skirts.
Princess Anne
Observer, 'Sayings of the Week', 18 September 1983

2   The success of a netball team comes largely from accurate passing.
Mary Bulloch
Basic Netball, 1957, Ch. VI

3   Why, when basketball attracts so many women followers, do not more men turn up for netball?
Louise Taylor
The Times, 26 November 1988

---

65 NEWSPAPERS

See also 97 Television

---

1   If there is anything tougher than a sports editor, I should not like to meet it.
Earl of Arran
House of Lords, 10 May 1962

2   I wanted to be a sports writer, but it took me too long to turn out my stuff. I found I could become Vice-President faster than I could become a newspaper man.
Richard Nixon
James Beasley Simpson, *Best Quotes of '54, '55, '56*, 1957

3   A sports writer is a guy who could get himself slugged regularly each Tuesday and Thursday if fist fighters, ball players, and such didn't have a commendable and wholly unreasonable awe for something called 'the power of the press'.
Red Smith
James Beasley Simpson, *Best Quotes of '54, '55, '56*, 1957

66 OLYMPIC GAMES

1   If only politicians had to sweat it out to get to the Olympics they might not be quite so keen to say to we sports people, 'Sorry, you're not going.'
Princess Anne
John Samuel, *The Guardian Book of Sports Quotes,* 1985

2   Some people wonder why fine arts should be in the Olympics. Why shouldn't they be? The Greeks had them. And sport itself is a fine art. Yes a fine art.
Avery Brundage
Sports Illustrated, 30 January 1957

3   The Olympic Movement is a twentieth-century religion. Where there is no injustice of caste, of race, of family, of wealth.
Avery Brundage
Jonathon Green, *A Dictionary of Contemporary Quotations,* 1982

4   [On turning back from a journey to Greece] I escaped the implication of being thought to have gone to the Olympic Games. That would have been disgraceful in any crisis of state, but in this one [the assassination of Caesar] it would have been inexcusable.
Marcus Tullius Cicero (106–43 BC)
Letter to Atticus, XVI, 7

5   The most important thing in the Olympic Games is not winning but taking part ... The essential thing in life is not conquering but fighting well.
Baron Pierre de Coubertin (1863–1937)
Speech, London, 24 July 1908

6   The biggest thing in any Olympics is to have self-confidence and belief. Mary [Rand] came in with her gold medal, threw it at me, and told me to go out there and get one. [He did.]
Lynn Davies
Independent, 18 October 1989

7   Everyone else who finishes second is disappointed. I don't agree. The Olympics are about performance, doing the best you can do.
Carl Lewis
New York Times, 24 September 1988

8   It's not like home, but I think the Olympics is about sportsmen being together.
Edwin Moses
Sunday Times, 29 July 1984

9   The Olympics is always an exercise in misery. Ten thousand people around the world start off thinking it is going to be them in two years but only one person ends up on the rostrum.
Pete Newlands
Sunday Times, 12 June 1988

10   It's good for the ego, being a small part of a big picture. If I come away [from the Olympics] with a medal, it would be the highlight of my year. If I came away with a gold, it would be the highlight of my life.
Pam Shriver
New York Times, 21 September 1988

11   At the Olympics I love watching almost anything at all that's special, as long as it doesn't have a horse in it.
Daley Thompson
Financial Times, 17 September 1988

67   ORIENTEERING

1   Orienteering is an education.
Bron Gösta 'Rak' Lagerfelt
Foreword to Gordon Pirie, *The Challenge of Orienteering,* 1986

2   Orienteering is a mixture of geography, map-reading, mathematics, intellect and character-training as well as physical education.
Gordon Pirie
The Challenge of Orienteering, 1986, Ch. 1

3   Orienteering is often likened to a car rally on foot.
Brian Porteus
Orienteering, 1978, Introduction

68 PARACHUTING

1 There are two thrills in a man's life and the second one is parachuting.
Anonymous (opinion attributed to members of the Parachute Regiment)
Observer, 23 November 1986

69 POLE VAULT

1 Pole vaulting is a religious experience.
Richard V. Ganslen
Mechanics of the Pole Vault, 8th ed., 1973

2 Keep arms straight, don't pull on the pole. I think 'go to sleep on the pole'.
Dave Roberts
Richard V. Ganslen, *Mechanics of the Pole Vault*, 9th ed., 1980

3 We may be getting near the maximum now, maximum hand grip, maximum speed, maximum technique – where else can you improve?
Keith Stock
Sunday Times, 19 July 1981

70 POLITICS

1 It [politics] is quieter, less controversial, more reflective and more physical [than sport].
Sebastian Coe
Independent, 'Quotes of the Week', 16 September 1989

2 It seems to us ironic that politicians are always quick to cash in on sporting success but not so quick to lend financial support.
Arthur McAllister
The Times, 1 January 1987

3   Being in politics is like being a football coach. You have to be smart enough to understand the game and dumb enough to think it's important.

Eugene McCarthy
Scholastic Coach, January 1989

4   Even if they have Nelson Mandela bowl the first ball of the tour and let him march to permanent freedom via the members' pavilion, this tour would still be a moral boost for the autocrats of apartheid.

Tom Rosenthal
Observer, 'Sayings of the Week', 20 August 1989

71 POLO

See also 105 Water Polo

1   Polo is horse hockey.

Anonymous

2   Polo is all I think about now. I still have business interests but resent having to waste a minute on them. Polo people are a fantastic group and I love their company; they wouldn't know what a takeover bid meant.

Kerry Packer
Sydney Morning Herald, 'Sayings of the Week', 18 February 1989

3   Those who have the money to purchase first-class horses cannot ride them, and who can ride them have not the money.

Andrew Barton Paterson (1864–1941)
Article on Polo in *Australian Magazine*, 6 July 1899
Clement Semmler, *The Banjo of the Bush*, 1966, Ch. 6

72 POWERBOAT RACING

1   Driving a powerboat is a bit like having one person throw a bucket of water over you while another hits you with a baseball bat.
Steve Curtis
Observer, 3 September 1989

2   The sport makes Formula One look tame.
Phil Duggan
Observer, 18 June 1989

73 RACING

See also 16 Chariot Racing
28 Drag Racing
41 Greyhound Racing
45 Harness Racing
61 Motor Racing
72 Powerboat Racing

1   A racehorse is the only horse which can take thousands of people for a ride at the same time.
Anonymous

2   If you don't run outsiders, outsiders can never win.
Anonymous

3   Horses and jockeys mature earlier than people – which is why horses are admitted to race tracks at the age of two, and jockeys before they are old enough to shave.
Dick Beddoes
Laurence J. Peter, *Peter's Quotations*, 1977

4   Horse-races are desports of great men, and good in themselves, though many gentlemen by such means gallop quite out of their fortunes.
Robert Burton (1577–1640)
Anatomy of Melancholy, 1660, Pt. II, Sec. 2, Ch. 4

5   He may be a bit older now, but he's still Lester Piggott. He won't give up until an arm falls off.
Willie Carson
Sunday Times, 18 October 1981

6   It's like making love every time I get on the horse [Nashwan].
Willie Carson
Independent, 'Quotes of the Week', 10 June 1989

7   The dieting is simple, but it's never easy. A jockey just has to accept it as part of his life.
Steve Cauthen
Sunday Times, 2 April 1989

8   It's a vital part of my riding that I try to understand the horse's mentality, and not just think about how fast I can go or whatever.
Steve Cauthen
Sunday Correspondent, 29 October 1989

9   I feel as a horse must feel when the beautiful cup is given to the jockey.
Edgar Degas (1834–1917) (on seeing one of his paintings sold)
Attributed

10   Don't misjudge the finish time, or you'll get a size 10½ in the rear.
Grover Delp
New York Times, 6 May 1979

11   Peter Scudamore is in one race and the rest of us are in another.
Mark Dwyer
Independent, 2 December 1988

12   There are more heartbreaks in racing than hoofbeats.
'Hollywood' George Edser
Sydney Morning Herald, 'Sayings of the Week', 13 July 1985

13   [Horse racing] is one of the real sports that's left to us: a bit of danger and a bit of excitement and the horses, which are the best thing in the world.
Queen Elizabeth, the Queen Mother
Observer, 'Sayings of the Week', 29 March 1987

14 I was always getting sand kicked in my face as a kid and now I'm getting paid for it.

Richard Fox (on 'kickback' – the material thrown up by horses' hooves, following the first British race meeting run on an artificial surface)
Independent, 31 October 1989

15 A good horseman wants a good spur.

Thomas Fuller (1654–1734)
Gnomologia, 1732, No. 155

16 A good horse should be seldom spurr'd.

Thomas Fuller (1654–1734)
Ibid., No. 157

17 Everyone knows that horse-racing is carried on mainly for the delight and profit of fools, ruffians, and thieves.

George Gissing (1857–1903)
The Private Papers of Henry Ryecroft, 1903

18 A hum of course cheering, a dense crowd careering,
   All sights seen obscurely, all shouts vaguely heard;
'The green wins!' 'The crimson!' The multitude swims on,
   And figures are blended and features are blurr'd.

'The horse is her master!' 'The green forges past her!'
   'The clown will outlast her!' 'The clown wins!' 'The clown!'
The white railing races with all the white faces,
   The chestnut outpaces, outstretches the brown.

On still past the gateway she strains in the straightway,
   Still struggles, 'The clown by a short neck at most,'
He swerves, the green scourges, the stand rocks and surges,
   And flashes, and verges, and flits the white post.

Adam Lindsay Gordon (1833–70)
How We Beat the Favourite

19 We're aggressive and competitive but we can't all be Desert Orchids, and loved by all.

Bobby Gould
Independent, 'Quotes of the Week', 25 March 1989

20 Horse-racing is the delight and ruin of numbers [of Britons].

William Hazlitt (1778–1830)
Merry England

21 Except by accident, the race-horse never trots. He must either walk or gallop; and in exercise, even when it is the hardest, the gallop begins slowly and gradually, and increases till the horse is nearly at full speed.

Thomas Holcroft (1745–1809)
Memoirs, 1816

22 Racing-horses are essentially gambling implements.

Oliver Wendell Holmes (1809–94)
The Autocrat of the Breakfast Table, 1858, Ch. II

23 Whenever the trotting horse goes, he carries in his train brisk omnibuses, lively bakers' carts, and therefore hot rolls, the jolly butcher's wagon, the cheerful gig, the wholesome afternoon drive with wife and child, – all the forms of moral excellence, except truth, which does not agree with any kind of horse-flesh. The racer brings with him gambling, cursing, swearing, drinking, and a distaste for mob-caps and the middle aged virtues.

Oliver Wendell Holmes (1809–94)
Ibid.

24 Did you ever go to a horse-race and lay your money on Sure Thing and never see the hard-earned again?

Elbert Hubbard (1856–1915)
Notebook, 1927, p. 49

25 Race problem: picking the winner.

Frank McKinney Hubbard (1868–1930)
The Roycroft Dictionary, 1923

26 Horse-racing would not be the exciting diversion it is unless the horses were, as they are, bred for the purpose – were, in fact, professionals. A match between a couple of dray horses would have little interest – except, perhaps for the horses themselves.

Illustrated Sporting and Dramatic News, 18 October 1890

27 All the speed is in the spurs.

James Kelly
Scottish Proverbs, 1721, A, No. 139

28 With a choice between a class horse and a class jockey I would take the horse every time.

D. Wayne Lukas
Independent, 6 May 1989

29　The last time there was a successful objection in a classic was in England, and all the stewards who sat on it were dead within the year.

Major Dermot McCalmont
The Times, 9 February 1987

30　It is unforgivable to deny racegoers the facilities for losing their money swiftly and painlessly.

Hugh McIlvanney
Observer, 13 October 1985

31　If a horse runs badly the trainer kicks the jockey, the jockey kicks the horse, they all kick the stable cat and then there's nobody left to kick except the handicapper.

Christopher Mordaunt
Sunday Times, 18 February 1990

32　There are, they say, fools, bloody fools, and men who remount in a steeplechase.

John Oaksey
Jonathon Green, *A Dictionary of Contemporary Quotations*, 1982

33　A racing horse is not like a machine. It has to be tuned up just like you tune up a racing car.

Chris Pool
Private Eye, No. 621, 4 October 1985

34　They're not really bookies these days, they're just debt collectors.

Jack Ramsden
Independent, 'Quotes of the Week', 14 October 1989

35　Race-riding is like driving in heavy traffic. You never want to get stuck behind a bus.

Michael Roberts
Independent, 'Quotes of the Week', 30 July 1988

36　We have found lots of people keen on racing but not knowing how to get in. As far as they were concerned, it consists of a bunch of men in green coats and brown trilbies saying 'water bottle, water bottle'.

David Robinson
Sunday Times, 23 May 1982

37   Slow horses never die.
Robert Sangster
Sunday Times, 24 June 1984

38   When those stalls open, the horses are literally going to explode.
Brough Scott, Channel 4
Private Eye, No. 725, 29 September 1989

39   If after I have retired I overhear a father saying to his son at the races, 'That's Peter Scudamore over there, now he *could* ride,' I will be more than content.
Peter Scudamore
Sunday Times, 12 March 1989

> 40   Being better hors'd
> Out-rode me.
> William Shakespeare (1564–1616)
> *Henry IV Pt. II*, 1597–8, Act I, Sc. I

41   For most people in this game, racing is their food and water.
Simon Sherwood
The Times, 19 November 1988

42   I just click my tongue at them when I want them to go.
Willie Shoemaker
The Times, 22 June 1984

43   At the Leith races, the best company comes hither from the remoter provinces.
Tobias Smollett (1721–71)
The Expedition of Humphrey Clinker, 1771, Vol. II

74 RECORDS

1   World records are like shirts. Anyone can have one if he works for it.
Filbert Bayi
John Samuel, *The Guardian Book of Sports Quotes*, 1985

75 REFEREES/UMPIRES

1   [Referees belong] to a sporting profession closely akin to that of a piano accompaniest to great singers. Do the job perfectly and everyone applauds the singer. Strike just one long note and everyone from the singer outwards scowls and accuses you of ruining the performance.

Anonymous referee
The Times, 19 February 1987

2   Integrity is what makes a good referee.... It's not *who* is right, but what is right.

Fred Burakat
Scholastic Coach, November 1988

3   You guys are like politicians. You're never right.

Gerald Ford (talking to umpires)
York Times, 16 July 1978

76 RODEOING

1   Rodeoing is about the only sport you can't fix. You'd have to talk to the bulls and the horses, and they wouldn't understand you.

Bill Linderman
James Beasley Simpson, *Best Quotes of '54, '55, '56*, 1957

2   It [rodeoing]'s not a sport you can practise by yourself. A bull will come after you when you are on the ground. You have to have people around you.

Bob Sheridan
New York Times, 29 September 1980

77 ROLLER SKATING

1   This should tell you something about the appeal of this sport [roller skating]. I'm married and have a daughter, but I gave up a good CPA [Certified Public Accountant] job with a top firm three years ago to devote full time to coaching skaters.
Jack Burton
New York Times, 17 June 1979

78 ROWING

1   Oarsmen do it back to front.
Anonymous

2   Rodney Bewes, a member of the London Rowing Club – that's one of the London clubs.
Harry Carpenter
Private Eye, No. 661, 17 April 1987

3   Your legs are on fire, your lungs are bursting and you think you can taste the blood. You shut the world out of your mind and row. You wonder where your boat is, where the other boats are. Something drives you on, to give more than you can give.
Tom Cattell
New York Times, 4 June 1978

4   When we [oarsmen] run with football players they drop out after a mile or two. We're in much better condition. We relate more to marathoners, cross-country skiers and cyclists.
Tom Cattell
Ibid.

5   One can never really row: one can only illustrate in a boat what one thinks rowing is.
Steve Fairbairn (1862–1938)
Ian Fairbairn (ed.), *Steve Fairbairn on Rowing*, 1951

6   Mileage makes champions.
Steve Fairbairn (1862–1938)
Ibid.

> 7   Once on a dim and dream-like shore
>   Half seen, half recollected,
>   I thought I met a human oar
>   Ideally perfected.
>   To me at least he seemed a man
>   Like any of our neighbours,
>   Formed on the self-same sort of plan
>   For high aquatic labours.
>   R. C. Lehmann (1856–1929)
>   *The Perfect Oar*

8   There is no doubt some truth in the Cambridge assertion that there are two races, one on the water and the other – who ends up with the most internationals.
Donald Macdonald (referring to the Oxford and Cambridge Boat Race)
Guardian, 31 January 1987

> 9   And all the way, to guide their chime,
>   With falling oars they kept the time.
>   Andrew Marvell (1621–78)
>   *Bermudas,* 1657

> 10   Faintly as tolls the evening chime,
>   Our voices keep tune and our oars keep time.
>   Thomas Moore (1779–1852)
>   *Poems Relating to America*

11   You don't have to be lovers to work well in a boat.
Dan Topolski
Independent, 'Quotes of the Olympic Games', 1 October 1988

79 RUGBY

See also 35 Football (American)

1   Because Rugby actively employs all the faculties it is the king among ball-games–and the hands, you might say, are the king of kings.

Fred Allen and Terry McLean
Fred Allen on Rugby, 1970, Ch. 5

2   The art of kicking is the capacity to believe in the possible.

Fred Allen and Terry McLean
Ibid., Ch. 8

3   Good goalkicking is a mixture of technique and temperament. You must try to box up the goalkicking in a little compartment away from everything else and become a little machine from the moment the whistle goes and a penalty is awarded.

Rob Andrew
Guardian, 4 March 1989

4   Give blood: play rugby.

Anonymous

5
THIS STONE
COMMEMORATES THE EXPLOIT OF
WILLIAM WEBB ELLIS
WHO WITH A FINE DISREGARD FOR THE RULES OF FOOTBALL
AS PLAYED IN HIS TIME
FIRST TOOK THE BALL IN HIS ARMS AND RAN WITH IT
THUS ORIGINATING THE DISTINCTIVE FEATURE OF
THE RUGBY GAME
AD 1823

Anonymous
Inscription on a marble tablet at Rugby School

6   We'll probably drink as hard as we train–that's very hard.

Stuart Barnes
Independent, 'Quotes of the Week', 18 March 1989

7   Get the ball out to the wing three-quarter, there's fewer players out there.

Carston Catcheside
The Times, 20 February 1987

8   I can't see any way the governing bodies can stop players being used when millions of pounds are being pumped into the game.
Gareth Davies
The Times, 6 September 1985

9   You'd never guess. I've bought you a Rugby League football team for an anniversary present.
Geoffrey Edelstein
Sydney Morning Herald, 'Sayings of the Week', 2 August 1986

10   It [rugby union] is the last amateur sport in the world. The only one which players still play for enjoyment, if they start to play for money it will cease to be enjoyment. It will simply be work.
Albert Ferrasse
The Times, 19 February 1987

11   Modern rugby players . . . like to get their retaliation in first.
Kim Fletcher
Sunday Times, 12 January 1986

12   Our [French rugby union] forwards seem to have forgotten that they also have to play as forwards.
Jacques Fouroux
Guardian, 15 March 1989

13   Psyching up Welsh players is no problem. The first boost comes when they're selected; putting the three feathers on their chest is then all they need. What I have to do is to quieten them down and that is why the most difficult area I work in is the position above the eyeballs.
Tony Gray (coach to the Welsh team)
The Times, 21 March 1987

14   League is much, much more physical than union, and that's before anyone starts breaking the rules.
Adrian Hadley
Independent, 'Quotes of the Week', 26 November 1988

15   Players in secure employment and happily married are always more consistent than the young tearaways.
William Henry 'Dusty' Hare
Sunday Telegraph, 9 April 1989

16   I'll be content to play the game from the stand, the easiest
position of all.

'Dusty' Hare (on retiring as an active player)
Daily Telegraph, 29 April 1989

17   If you run you *make* gaps. To do that, you need people to be
alert. You need quick ball. It's quick hands that make the overlap.
But the thing is, the whole team must work for it.

Mike Harrison
The Times, 20 February 1987

18   If you sent everyone off for punching, we'd have nobody left
playing the game. I think we've all punched on a rugby pitch,
haven't we?

Colin High
Guardian, 7 February 1987

19   The bigger the crowd the more I enjoy it.

Richard Hill
The Times, 7 June 1984

20   They came to a sort of gigantic gallows of two poles eighteen
feet high, fixed upright in the ground some fourteen feet apart
with a cross-bar running from one to the other at the height of ten
feet or thereabouts.

Thomas Hughes (1822–96)
Tom Brown's Schooldays, 1857, Pt. I, Ch. V

21   The match is for the best of three goals; whichever side kicks
two goals wins, and it won't do, you see, just to kick the ball
through these posts, it must go over the cross-bar; any height'll do,
so long as it's between the posts. You'll have to stay in goal to touch
the ball when it rolls behind the posts, because if the other side
touch it they have a try at goal.

Thomas Hughes (1822–96)
Ibid.

22   You say, you don't see much in it at all, nothing but a
struggling mass of boys, and a leather ball, which seems to excite
them all to great fury, as a red rag does a bull. My dear sir, a battle
would look much the same to you, except that the boys would be
men, and the balls iron.

Thomas Hughes (1822–96)
Ibid.

23 Rugby is a physical game and there is no place for the delicate sex.

John Jeavons-Fellows
The Times, 1 January 1987

24 'Good ball' is another coaching term that seems to have applied blinkers to some of our players . . . I believe a 'good ball' is when my side have the ball and 'bad ball' is when the opposition have it!

Dick Jeeps
The Times, 20 February 1987

25 The best part of the game is running up the pitch with the ball in your hand.

John Jeffrey
Guardian, 20 February 1987

26 Backs are the poets in motion of rugby, and all the excitement occurs when they are engaged.

Russell Celyn Jones
Observer, Colour Supplement, 1 February 1987

27 People have been criticizing [rugby league] referees since the game began in 1895 and a colleague has a copy of a newspaper from 1938 saying that standards of refereeing in that year were at their lowest ever.

Gerry Kershaw
The Times, 19 February 1987

28 I love what rugby is—brain as well as brawn, and then beer together afterwards. There's no other sport which caters for all shapes and sizes, or where players and spectators mix together so naturally after a match.

Roy Laidlaw
The Times, 19 March 1987

29 Twickenham's just a building until it's filled up with fans.

Dewi Morris
Sunday Times, 6 November 1988

30   League players tackle about twice as hard as they do in union.

Alex Murphy
Financial Times, 27 February 1988

31   After 162 years, rugby union still doesn't know what it wants to be when it grows up.

Geoffrey Nicholson
Observer, 8 September 1985

32   There's just one more rugby league result to give you, just to put the jigsaw into focus.

Andy Peebles
Private Eye, No. 636, 2 May 1986

33   [The ball] is specially shaped like a lozenge so it cannot roll, bounce properly or do any of the things for which a ball was designed.

Stephen Pile
Sunday Times, 29 September 1985

34   This sport is supposed to be about controlled aggression; perhaps I just control mine better than most.

Roy Powell
Sunday Telegraph, 'Quotes 1989', 24 December 1989

35   An All Black side doesn't have star players individually, there's just one star out there for them and that's the team itself.

Graham Price
Guardian, 14 October 1989

36   [Forwards are] like boxers, like rutting stags.

Ray Prosser
Observer, Colour Supplement, 1 February 1987

37   People say that players need to play in a vacuum but what is the point when you want them to go from that kind of atmosphere and play in front of 60 000 screaming Welshmen?

Keith Richardson
Independent, 6 May 1989

38   Rugby is based on one very simple idea . . . that each player should be as free as possible to get the ball and help his side score with it.

Derek Robinson
Rugby: Success Starts Here, 1969, Introduction

39   This is the beauty of the game. A bunch of players, sticking together, knowing, deep down, what they are capable of.

John Ryan
Daily Telegraph, 15 March 1989

40   Dirty play should never be condoned. Nor should softness.

John Scott
Weekend Guardian, 18–19 March 1989

41   Experience has conclusively shown that whatever be the class of the players, rugby cup-ties give an opening for ill-feeling and the exhibition of unnecessary roughness.

Sir Montague Shearman (1857–1930)
Athletics and Football, 1887

42   Anyone who doesn't watch rugby league is not a real person. He's a cow's hoof, an ethnic, senile or comes from Melbourne.

John Singleton
Australian, 12 December 1981
Bill Wannan, *Great Aussie Quotes*, 1982

43   It was about par for a rugby dinner . . . from what I can remember.

Colin Smart
Observer, 'Sayings of the Year', 19 December 1982

44   That's the amazing thing about team games; you can play in a match against your best mate and with a total stranger. But for that eighty minutes the total stranger is your very best mate in the world and your lifelong friend becomes the enemy.

Brian Smith
Guardian, 18 November 1989

45   We're serious and we are social. That's part of what's so great about rugby.

Raul Socher
New York Times, 4 May 1986

46   I have always thought the friendship you get out of rugby is the only thing money cannot buy.

Mike Teague
Independent, 'Quotes of the Week', 22 July 1989

47   Violence on the rugby field is a bore.

Denis Thatcher
The Times, 1 January 1987

48   You don't have violence in rugby league. Rugby league is a hooligan's game played by gentlemen and soccer is a gentleman's game played by hooligans.

Freddie Trueman
Sydney Morning Herald, 'Sayings of the Week', 24 August 1985

49   Rugby is a game which, in 99 cases out of 100, must have been played to be really understood.

H. B. T. Wakelam
Twickenham Calling, 1930, Introduction

50   It is very curious to notice in international football how large a part the national temperament plays on the field.

H. B. T. Wakelam
Ibid., Ch. VII

51   Rugby league players are a sterling bunch who for little or no financial reward are cheerfully prepared to undergo every cerebral experience from mild concussion to a profound coma in the interests of their sport.

Julie Welch
Observer, 25 March 1985

52   The fraternal spirit which exists in rugby union has a lot to do with the game being amateur.

Dudley Wood
Observer, 19 March 1989

80 RUNNING

See also 50 Hurdles
53 Jogging
58 Marathon

1   Distance runners keep it up longer.
Anonymous

2   Naturally, we wanted to achieve the honour of doing it first, but the main essence of sport is a race against opponents rather than against clocks.
Roger Bannister (having run a mile in less than four minutes on 6 May 1954)
James Beasley Simpson, *Best Quotes of '54, '55, '56*, 1957

3   I felt suddenly and gloriously free of the burden of athletic ambition that I had been carrying for years. No words could be invented for such supreme happiness, eclipsing all other feelings. I thought at that moment I could never again reach such a climax of single-mindedness.
Roger Bannister (on recalling his four-minute mile achieved twenty years before)
New York Times, 6 May 1979

4   Running has given me a glimpse of the greatest freedom that a man can ever know, because it results in the simultaneous liberation of both mind and body.
Roger Bannister
Jonathon Green, *A Dictionary of Contemporary Quotations*, 1982

5   Rejoiceth as a strong man to run a race.
Bible, Authorized Version
Psalms, I, Ch. 19, v. 5

6   Know ye not that they which run in a race run all, but one receiveth the prize?
Bible, Authorized Version
I Corinthians, Ch. 9, v. 24

7   Let us run with patience the race that is set before us.
Bible, Authorized Version
Hebrews, Ch. 12, v. 1

8   I'm just a girl who runs.
Zola Budd
Observer, 'Sayings of the Week', 29 April 1984

9   It behoves us to run in a watchful mode.
Frank Carlucci
Financial Times, 6 August 1988

10   When a man is running a race he should use all his strength and do all he can to win, but he should never use his foot to trip a competitor or his hand to foul him.
Chrysippus (third century BC)
Cicero, *De Officii*, III, x, 42

11   The brave and wise man does not groan aloud, except perhaps to make an intense effort, as when runners in the stadium shout as loudly as they can.
Marcus Tullius Cicero (106–43 BC)
Disputations, II, xxiv

12   Never tackle your secondary event before your first one.
Ron Clarke
Attributed

13   It may sound arrogant but I feel I have been the best 800 metres runner in the world since 1978.
Sebastian Coe
Observer, 'Sayings of the Week', 31 August 1986

14   And the line-up for the final of the Women's 400 metres hurdles includes three Russians, two East Germans, a Pole, a Swede and a Frenchman.
David Coleman
Private Eye, No. 542, 24 September 1982

15   That's the fastest time ever run – but it's not as fast as the world record.
David Coleman
Private Eye, No. 592, 24 August 1984

16   Nobody's unbeatable.
Steve Cram
New York Times, 22 September 1988

17   When the pace is slow like this, sometimes the athletes will make a move they hadn't planned to make, earlier in the race than they planned to do it.
Brendan Foster
Private Eye, No. 659, 20 March 1987

18   Running for money and running for performance are contradictory.

Brendan Foster
New York Times, 13 September 1988

19   He did a lot of running with his legs today.

Brendan Foster
Private Eye, No. 700, 14 October 1988

20   He's doing well . . . he's letting his legs do the running.

Brendan Foster
Private Eye, No. 716, 26 May 1989

21   He may well win the race that runs by himself.

Benjamin Franklin (1706–90)
Poor Richard's Almanac, 1757

22   I lift and reach out when I run, more like a guy than a girl.

Florence Griffith Joyner
Independent, 'Quotes of the Olympic Games', 1 October 1988

23   I would like to see them have races for men and women together. If I could race against Carl Lewis and Ben Johnson, I'd run 10.2.

Florence Griffith Joyner
The Times, 1 July 1989

24   My body is happy I retired. It went into shock. I didn't know what it was not to get up at five in the morning and have training all day.

Florence Griffith Joyner
Independent, 29 July 1989

25   There is a theory that if you enjoy cross-country running you can thrive on almost any kind of pain.

Peter Hildreth
Sunday Telegraph, 22 March 1987

26   Running for money doesn't make you run fast. It makes you run first.

Ben Jipcho
Jonathon Green, *A Dictionary of Contemporary Quotations*, 1982

27   Steven Cram may appear cool and relaxed, but inside there burns a heart of steel.

David Moorecroft, BBC Radio 4
Private Eye, No. 696, 19 August 1988

28   Thus far we run before the wind.

Arthur Murphy (c. 1727–1805)
The Apprentice, 1756, Act I, Sc. I

29   Zola Budd: so small, so waif-like, you literally can't see her. But there she is.

Alan Parry
Private Eye, No. 634, 4 April 1986

30   Steve Ovett, Sebastian Coe, Steve Cram – the vanguard of our cream.

Ron Pickering
Private Eye, No. 582, 6 April 1984

31   Watch the time – it gives you a good indication of how fast they are running.

Ron Pickering
Private Eye, No. 6, March 1987

32   We may outrun,
         By violent swiftness, that which we run at,
         And lose by over-running.

         William Shakespeare (1564–1616)
         Henry VIII, 1612–13, Act I, Sc. I

33   We have not heard the last word on running.

Alfred Shrubb (in 1908)
Brian Mitchell, *Running to Keep Fit*, 1984

34   I don't run in traffic very well.

Mary Decker Slaney
New York Times, 26 September 1988

35   We swing ungirded hips,
         And lightened are our eyes,
         The rain is on our lips,
         We do not run for prize.

         Charles Hamilton Sorley (1895–1915)
         The Song of the Ungirt Runners

36   There is no kind of exercise that has more uniformly met the approbation of authors in general than running. In the Middle Ages, foot-racing was considered as an essential part of a young man's education, especially if he was the son of a man of rank, and brought up to a military profession.
Joseph Strutt (1749–1802)
The Sports and Pastimes of the People of England, 1801, Bk. II, Ch. II, XI

37   And Cram's ankle injury is another headache the selectors could do without.
'Tony', GWR Sport
Private Eye, No. 722, 18 August 1989

38   There are even medical experts who think women are more compatible than men with long-distance running because they have less muscle and more endurance.
George Vecsey
New York Times, 4 August 1984

39   When the gun goes, you become a different human being.
Allan Wells
Observer, 'Sayings of the Week', 16 August 1981

40   He's running on his nerve ends.
Peter West
Private Eye, No. 580, 9 March 1984

41   Running is the most primitive form of athletic endeavour regarded as a sport.
Fred Wilt
Run Run Run, 1964, Introduction

81   SAILING

1   The mistakes and errors are the price for the great romance of doing something for the first time.
Sir Francis Chichester (1902–72)
The Lonely Sea and the Sky, 1964, Pt. V, Ch. 27

2   Sailing, like living, is so easy with the wind behind you.

Hunter Davies
Punch, 25 September 1985

3   Britain's glorious past in sailing plays against its future. The connotations of pink gins and white trousers are unacceptable to the average person.

Nigel Irens
Sunday Times, 5 June 1988

4   The sea is a challenge in itself and I can never be far from it.

Robin Knox-Johnston
Guardian, 23 September 1989

5   Any man who has to ask about the annual upkeep of a yacht can't afford one.

J. P. Morgan (1837–1913)
Clifton Fadiman, *The American Treasury: 1455–1955*, 1955

6   You can do business with anyone, but you can only sail a boat with a gentleman.

J. P. Morgan (1837–1913)
Ibid.

7   This [the America's Cup] is a big boys' game. Big bucks. Big egos. Big stakes, so big risks.

Peter de Savary
Independent, 'Quotes of the Week', 9 July 1988

82   SHOOTING

1   The grouse are in absolutely no danger from people who shoot grouse.

Duke of Edinburgh
Private Eye, No. 693, 8 July 1988

2   He that's always shooting, must sometimes hit.

Thomas Fuller (1654–1734)
Gnomologia, 1732, No. 2276

3   I had never practised shooting with ball; I had frightened a few snipe, and wounded a few partridges, but that was the extent of my experience. I know, however, that I could not possibly shoot worse than everybody else had done, and might by accident shoot better.
Thomas Chandler Haliburton (1796–1865)
The Attaché: or, Sam Slick in England, 1843, Vol. I, Ch. I

4   You should never go snipe-shooting when there are bears in sight.
Frank McKinney Hubbard (1868–1930)
Epigrams, 1923

5   On the First of September, one Sunday morn,
I shot a hen pheasant in standing corn
Without a licence. Contrive who can
Such a cluster of crimes against God and man!
Richard Monckton Milnes, Lord Houghton (1809–85)
The Crime

83   SHOWJUMPING

See also 30 Equestrianism
73 Racing

1   To win is everything. To be second is even worse than being secondary.
David Broome
Jonathon Green, *A Dictionary of Contemporary Quotations,* 1982

2   A rider can hype himself up to produce something extra, but how do you tell a horse it's that important? He's more interested in his dinner.
Ian Millar
Sunday Telegraph, 16 April 1989

3   These American horses know the fences like the back of their hands.
Harvey Smith
Private Eye, No. 678, 11 December 1987

4   It would be wrong for me to disclose how much showjumpers earn since it could bring about Inland Revenue problems.
Jack Webber
John Samuel, *The Guardian Book of Sports Quotes*, 1985

---

84   SKATEBOARDING

---

1   A skateboard at heart is a short thin plank with four wheels under it, a kind of elongated roller skate . . . It is a water ski for dry land, a snow ski for asphalt.
David Hunn
Skateboarding, 1977, Ch. 1

---

85   SKATING

---

1   Torvill and Dean move as if they are four legs attached.
Anonymous
Sandra Stevenson, *The BBC Book of Skating*, 1984, Ch. 6

2   Skaters, even when competing, need to have some form of dramatic quality within them.
Robin Cousins with David Foot
Skateaway, 1984, 'Confidential Asides'

3   'Stop, Sam stop!' said Mr Winkle, trembling violently, and clutching hold of Sam's arms with the grasp of a drowning man. 'How slippery it is, Sam!'
   'Not an uncommon thing upon ice, sir,' replied Mr Weller.
Charles Dickens (1812–70)
Pickwick Papers, 1836–37, Vol. II, Ch. 2

4   In skating over thin ice our safety is in our speed.
Ralph Waldo Emerson (1803–82)
Essays: First Series, 1841, 'Prudence'

5   Skating is a chilly pleasure, and therefore no sin.
Heinrich Heine (1797–1856)
Religion and Philosophy, 1882

6   All my life I have wanted to skate and all my life I have skated.
Sonja Henie
Wings on My Feet, 1940

7   When you've seen one skater, you've really seen the lot.
Ludovic Kennedy
Observer, 'Sayings of the Week', 1 April 1984

8   Society is like a large piece of frozen water; and skating well is the great art of social life.
Letitia Elizabeth Landon (1802–38)
Attributed

9   Then over the Parke . . . where I first in my life, it being a great frost, did see people sliding with their skeates, which is a very pretty art.
Samuel Pepys (1633–1703)
Diary, 1 December 1662

10   This speed skating is taking place virtually in the shadow of the Olympic flame.
Ron Pickering
Private Eye, No. 580, 9 March 1984

11   O'er the ice the rapid skater flies.
         With sport above and death below,
      Where mischief lurks in gay disguise
         Thus lightly touch and quickly go.
Pierre Charles Roy (1683–1764)
Lines appearing under a picture of skaters by Lancret, translated by Samuel Johnson

12   You've got to think of training beginning at six in the morning and going through to early afternoon daily. This really makes champions tick.
Stuart Russell
Sunday Telegraph, 26 March 1989

13   You cannot learn to skate without being ridiculous.
George Bernard Shaw (1856–1950)
Fanny's First Play, 1911, Introduction

14   If skaters want to criticize other ice dancers [couples] they say there was room to fit another person between them.

Sandra Stevenson
The BBC Book of Skating, 1984, Ch. 6

15   And in the frosty season, when the sun
Was set, and visible for many a mile
The cottage windows blazed through twilight gloom,
I heeded not their summons: happy time
It was indeed for all of us–for me
It was a time of rapture! Clear and loud
The village clock tolled six–I wheeled about
Proud and exulting like an untried horse
That cares not for his home. All shod with steel,
We hissed along the polished ice in games
Confederate, imitative of the chase
And woodland pleasures.

William Wordsworth (1770–1850)
'Skating', *The Prelude*

86   SKIING

1   A skilful skier is one who sets realistic objectives and who has a learned ability to achieve them effectively, efficiently and consistently under a wide range of environmental conditions.

Anonymous British coach
Punch, 25 September 1985

2   S ki in control
K eep clear of others
I f stopping, get out of the way

S top before you reach the lift line
A lways use ski brakes or straps
F ollow warning signs
E nter runs with care

Anonymous
Ski field notice board

3   When I first went skiing I broke a leg. Fortunately it wasn't mine.
Anonymous

4   If I had landed on my skis instead of my face it would have been a record jump.
Eddie 'The Eagle' Edwards
Sunday Correspondent, 31 December 1989

5   Avalanches are things that happen to other people in the resorts you never go to.
Mark Heller
Ski, 1969, Ch. 16

6   Every ski-tourist has his own stock of avalanche stories, as every angler treats everybody from his chest of wonderful catches.
Axel Heyst
The White Frenzy, no date, Ch. 24

7   I don't think anyone has *lived* until they have been on skis.
Andrew Irvine
Peter Lunn in *BBC Going Skiing*, Ch. 1

8   Skiing is a battle against yourself, always to the frontiers of the impossible. But most of all, it must give you pleasure. It is not an obligation but a joy.
Jean-Claude Killy
Sports Illustrated, 18 November 1968

9   There are no amateurs any more. To be good a skier must literally devote from four to six years of his life to the sport. You don't have time for school or a job, and you must travel the world. That's hard to do without compensation.
Jean-Claude Killy
John Samuel, *The Guardian Book of Sports Quotes*, 1985

10   Skiing is different than, say, a football game, which lasts for about two and a half hours and then it's over. In skiing it's a four-day affair. Like a chess game, one mistake in any of our four events and you may find your king is not only being checkmated but also captured.
Chip LaCasse
New York Times, 9 March 1980

11 There's nothing like skiing to open your eyes to the inexhaustible beauty of the world.
Sir Arnold Lunn
Axel Heyst, *The White Frenzy*, no date, Ch. 2

12 The purpose of skiing is to increase the sum total of fun.
Sir Arnold Lunn
John Shedden in *BBC Going Skiing*, Ch. 3

13 Skiing has been described as not so much a sport as a way of life.
Peter Lunn
'Skiing–A Love Affair' in *BBC Going Skiing*, 1984

14 The downhill is for weightlifters. The slalom is for gymnasts.
Hermann Nogler
Sunday Times, 6 February 1978

15 I don't race for records but because I deeply enjoy skiing.
Vreni Schneider
Daily Telegraph, 9 March 1989

16 The art of skiing is the art of turning, and the art of turning consists of shifting your weight on to the correct ski.
Maurice Tugwell
Skiing for Beginners, 1977

17 I did not learn so much before skiing. Now I want time to learn about life.
Pirmin Zurbriggen
Independent, 'Quotes of the Week', 11 February 1989

87 SKITTLES

1 He's up to these grand games, but one of these days I'll loore him on to skittles, and astonish him.
Henry James Byron (1834–84)
Our Boys, 1875 Act II

2   Life is with such all beer and skittles;
    They are not difficult to please
    About their victuals.
    Charles Stuart Calverley (1831–84)
    Contentment

3   *They* don't mind it; it's a regular holiday to them – all porter and skittles.
Charles Dickens (1812–70)
Pickwick Papers, 1836–37, Ch. 41

4   Life ain't all beer and skittles, and more's the pity; but what's the odds so long as you're happy?
George B. Du Maurier (1834–96)
Trilby, 1894, Pt. I

5   Life isn't all beer and skittles – but beer and skittles, or something better of the same sort, must form a good part of every Englishman's education.
Thomas Hughes (1822–96)
Tom Brown's Schooldays, 1857, Pt. I, Ch. II

88   SNOOKER

See also 9 Billiards

1   In snooker you play the balls not your opponent.
Anonymous

2   Q. Why are the players wearing dress suits in the afternoon?
    A. Because they've come prepared to play all night.
Anonymous
Observer, 1 February 1987

3   Playing snooker gives you firm hands and helps to build up character. It is the ideal recreation for dedicated nuns.
Archbishop Luigi Barbarito
Observer, 'Sayings of the Week', 19 November 1989

4   I'm a professional snooker player and I'm playing to win. If the fans don't like it, they can lump it.

Eddie Charlton
Guardian, 20 April 1989

5   Women are always asking for photographs of me leaning over the snooker table. It's my bottom they want to look at.

Steve Davis
Observer, 'Sayings of the Week', 16 May 1982

6   Snooker without the money and publicity would be like bar billiards.

Steve Davis
Sunday Times, 9 April 1989

7   The fascination and frustration of snooker is that you just don't know how you're going to play.

Steve Davis
The Times, 14 April 1989

8   Why snooker is still an obsession I'm not too sure. If you look at it one way, I've got nothing else to do.

Steve Davis
Observer, 'Sayings of the Week', 16 April 1989

9   Whoever wins the first frame will be one frame up.

Steve Davis
Private Eye, No. 734, 2 February 1990

10   People talk about the pressure in the game. But give me the pressure – compared to the jobs I used to do, this is money for old rope.

Terry Griffiths
Observer, 'Quotes of the Year', 19 December 1982

11   Steve Davis is trailing by one frame, so the pressure is balanced on him.

Rex Harris
Private Eye, No. 627, 27 December 1985

12   Can snooker live without me?

Alex Higgins
Observer, 'Sayings of the Week', 30 November 1986

13   It takes twenty years to become an institution.
Alex Higgins
Sunday Times, 12 March 1989

14   I dream all the time and suddenly it's true.
Joe Johnson (on winning the World Snooker Championship)
Observer, 'Sayings of the Week', 11 May 1986

15   Oh and that's a brilliant shot, the odd thing is that his mum's
not very keen on snooker.
Ted Lowe
Private Eye, No. 542, 24 September 1982

16   And for those of you watching this in black and white, the
pink sits behind the yellow.
Ted Lowe
Observer, 2 February 1986

17   Fred Davis, the doyen of snooker, now sixty-seven years of
age and too old to get his leg over, prefers to use his left hand.
Ted Lowe
Ibid.

18   They're not only snooker players, they're engineers, taking
apart a snooker cue and screwing it back again.
Ted Lowe
Private Eye, No. 679, 25 December 1987

19   Of course, one of Stephen Hendry's greatest assets is his
ability to score when he's playing.
Ted Lowe
Private Eye, No. 681, 22 January 1988

20   At his best, Mountjoy wasn't as good as he is now.
Ted Lowe
Private Eye, No. 709, 17 February 1989

21   Steve Davis – acknowledged by his peers to be the peerless
master.
John McCririck
Private Eye, No. 6, March 1987

22   You've got to remember that the snooker season is not a five-furlong sprint, it is a Gold Cup course. It only takes a couple of defeats for people to start writing you off.

John Parrott
The Times, 14 October 1989

23   I used to enjoy the Crucible; once it was fun. Now it is all a business.

Ray Reardon
Sunday Telegraph, 23 April 1989

24   He has to stay level, or one frame behind, that's the only way he can beat him.

Dennis Taylor
Private Eye, No. 602, 25 January 1985

25   After twelve frames, they stand all square. The next frame, believe it or not, is the thirteenth.

David Vine
Private Eye, No. 603, 7 February 1986

26   That's the sportsmanship you find in snooker, Terry asked Jimmy for a rub of his sandpaper.

John Virgo
Private Eye, No. 689, 13 May 1988

27   Terry Griffiths once very kindly advised me to alter my cue action. I listened, nodded politely, and did nothing. I try not to think about my technique too much. It is your cue that hits the ball, not your head.

Jimmy Wattana
Observer, 15 October 1989

28   I used to treat the top players with too much respect but everybody is there for the taking – as long as you knock the balls in.

Gary Wilkinson
The Times, 14 October 1989

29   An idiot can become a great snooker player but he is still an idiot.

Rex Williams
The Times, 14 October 1989

30   I hope he [Barry Hearn] never goes out of snooker because
the only job he'd want is God's.
Cliff Wilson
Independent, 21 October 1988

---

89   SPONSORSHIP

---

1   Sponsorship is the hardest part for everyone.
Robin Knox-Johnston
The Times, 12 January 1989

2   At Crystal Palace the BBC camera picked up a solemn lady
called Paula Fudge as she pounded along a running track with
BRITISH MEAT written across her understandably heaving
bosom. Sponsorship in sport is one thing but this was altogether a
different kettle of offal.
Dennis Potter
John Samuel, *The Guardian Book of Sports Quotes,* 1985

---

90   SPORT

---

1   A Sportsman is a man who does not boast;
      nor quit; nor make excuses when he fails.
   He is a cheerful loser, and a quiet winner.
   He plays fair and as well as he can.
   He enjoys the pleasure of risk.
   He gives his opponent the benefit of the doubt and he values
      the game itself more highly than the result.
Anonymous
Margaret Boyd, *Lacrosse: Playing and Coaching,* 1959

2   For what do we live, but to make sport for our neighbours, and
laugh at them in our turn?
Jane Austen (1775–1817)
Pride and Prejudice, 1813, Ch. 57

3   There is a need to feel our bodies have a skill and energy of their own, apart from the man-made machines they drive. There is the desire to find in sport a companionship with kindred people. I have found all these.
Roger Bannister
James Beasley Simpson, *Best Quotes of '54, '55, '56*, 1957

4   We who encourage sport cannot encourage it as something that is good for you, just as it wouldn't do for us to say to listen to music because it does you good. Rather, we must encourage it as fun, which it is.
Roger Bannister
New York Times, 6 May 1979

5   Just as businessmen get ulcers through business, so sportsmen must expect to suffer the strain of their work in sport.
Ken Barrington
Playing It Straight, 1968, Ch. 13

6   Sport is a wonderfully democratic thing, one of the few honourable battlefields left.
Danny Blanchflower
Jonathon Green, *A Dictionary of Contemporary Quotations*, 1982

7   Many other sports and recreations there be, much in use, as ringing, bowling, shooting . . . keelpins, trunks, quoits, pitching bars, hurling, wrestling, leaping, running, fencing, mustering, swimming, wasters, foils, football, ballon quintain etc., and many such, which are the common recreations of the country folks; riding of great horses, running at rings, tilts and tournaments, horse races, wild-goose chases, which are the disports of greater men, and good in themselves, though many gentlemen by that means gallop quite out of their fortunes.
Robert Burton (1577–1640)
The Anatomy of Melancholy, Pt. II, Sec. II

8   Sport is hard work for which you do not get paid.
Irvin S. Cobb
Laurence J. Peter, *Peter's Quotation*, 1977

9   Positive results in sport are magnified, but so are negative results. Failure breeds failure.
Sebastian Coe
The Times, 1 August 1984

10   Sports is the toy department of human life.

Howard Cosell
Barbara Rowes, *The Book of Quotes*, 1979

11   We take sport much too seriously and for all the wrong reasons.

Duke of Edinburgh
Observer, 'Sayings of the Week', 21 April 1985

12   The way sport has developed in this country [UK] is a matter of history and it is really quite impossible to attempt to wipe it all out and start again.

Duke of Edinburgh
The Times, 20 May 1986

13   The path of a successful sportsman is never a smooth one.

Jack Fingleton
Batting From Memory, 1981, Ch. 8

14   Sport is the most unifying influence in the world today.

Sir Denis Follows
Observer, 'Sayings of the Week', 9 March 1980

15   Wild animals never kill for sport.

James Anthony Froude (1818–94)
Oceana, 1886, Ch. 5

16   Sport, in a sense, is its own religion.

Duncan Goodhew
Sunday Times, 20 September 1981

17   The thing with sport, any sport, is that swearing is very much part of it.

Jimmy Greaves
Observer, 'Sayings of the Week', 21 February 1989

18   Every sportsman knows that Fate or Lady Luck, or whatever you may wish to call her, plays a big part in his career.

Reg Harris with G. H. Bowden
Two Wheels to the Top, 1976, Ch. 5

19   There is no better place [than England] where trap-ball, fives, prison base, football, quoits, bowls are better understood or more successfully practised . . . Then again cudgel-playing, quarter-staff, bull and badger-baiting, cock fighting are almost the peculiar diversions of this island, and often objected to as barbarous and cruel.

William Hazlitt (1778–1830)
Merry England

20   To brag little, – to show well, – to crow gently, if in luck, – to pay up, to own up, and to shut up, if beaten, are the virtues of a sporting man.

Oliver Wendell Holmes (1809–94)
The Autocrat of the Breakfast Table, 1858, Ch. II

21   Even our sports are dangers!

Ben Jonson (c. 1573–1637)
Underwoods, 1640

22   He that cannot make sport, should mar none.

James Kelly
Scottish Proverbs, 1721, H, No. 126

23   It is a good sport that fills the belly.

James Kelly
Ibid., I, No. 103

24   There is no sport where there is neither old folk nor bairns.

James Kelly
Ibid., T, No. 240

25   Then ye returned to your trinkets; then ye contented your
            souls
        With the flannelled fools at the wicket or the muddied oafs at
            the goals.

    Rudyard Kipling (1865–1936)
    The Islanders

26   All of sport, from bushkazi to baseball, is man's endeavour to balance his animal instinct against his civilizing intellect. On the sporting field . . . we are both ape and angel.

Christy Mathewson
New York Times, 25 June 1983

27 Sport has long since passed the stage when it was only a pastime.
Willy Meisl
'The Importance of Being Amateur' in Alex Natan (ed.), *Sport and Society*, 1958

28 I hate all sports as rabidly as a person who likes sports hates common sense.
H. L. Mencken (1880–1956)
Laurence J. Peter, *Peter's Quotations*, 1977

29 Sports is a feature documentary about national hysteria.
Keith Miles
The Finest Swordsman in All France: A Celebration of the Cliché, 1984

30 Attitudes in sport are mere echoes of what is happening in society.
Michael Parkinson
Introduction to Jack Fingleton, *Cricket Crisis*, 1984

31 We lose many young women to sport when they leave school because of boyfriends, discos and the belief that it's unglamorous to sweat or to get your hair wet.
Mary Peters
Observer, 25 June 1989

32 As I emphatically disbelieve in seeing Harvard or any other college turn out mollycoddles instead of vigorous men, I may add that I do not in the least object to a sport because it is rough.
Theodore Roosevelt (1858–1919)
Speech, 1907

33 Sport is such a pervasive human activity that to ignore it is to overlook one of the most significant aspects of contemporary American society.
George Sage
Sport and American Society, 1974

34 He who believes in education, criminal law, and sport, needs only property to make his a perfect modern gentleman.
George Bernard Shaw (1856–1950)
Maxims for Revolutionists, 1903

35   When a man wants to murder a tiger he calls it sport: when the tiger wants to murder him he calls it ferocity.
George Bernard Shaw (1856–1950)
Ibid.

36   All tours, whatever the sport, whatever the country, are train, sleep, play and eat.
Paul Stimpson
Sunday Times, 31 May 1981

37   Sport is imposing order on what was chaos.
Anthony Storr
Jonathon Green, *A Dictionary of Contemporary Quotations*, 1982

38   Some local education authorities actually think competitive sport is bad for children. They'll be telling us next that water doesn't suit goldfish.
Dick Tracey
The Times, 1 January 1987

39   [Man] is the only creature that inflicts pain for sport, knowing it to *be* pain.
Mark Twain (1835–1910)
Autobiography, 1908, Vol. II

40   I am afraid I play no outdoor games at all, except dominoes. I have sometimes played dominoes outside French cafés.
Oscar Wilde (1854–1900)
Rudolf Flesch, *The Book of Unusual Quotations*, 1959

---

91   SQUASH

---

1   One of the advantages of squash is that if you cannot find an opponent you can always play with yourself.
Anonymous

2   Remarkable – but would it not be possible to arrange two coolies to do this for you?
Anonymous Chinese (on being shown the game of squash)
Brian Phillips, *Tackle Squash Rackets This Way*, 1960, Ch. 1

3   Squash is nothing more than banging a ball about in a box.
Anonymous

4   Squash is not a game, it is a perversion.
Anonymous
Alan Colburn, *Squash: The Ambitious Player's Guide*, 1981, Ch. 16

5   Squash players do it against the wall.
Anonymous

6   Length is what the game of squash is all about.
Jonah Barrington
Barrington on Squash, 1973, Lesson 15

7   There have been many great 'thinkers' off the court but too
few in the actual game of 'physical chess'.
Jonah Barrington
Ibid., Lesson 36

8   Squash is a game of vicious movements, of leaps and darts and
lunges.
Jonah Barrington with John Hopkins
Tackle Squash, 1976, Introduction

9   In detail, squash is a very boring game. How many ways can
you tell people how to hit the ball on to that front wall.
Jonah Barrington
Ross Reyburn and Michael Emery, *Jonah*, 1983, Ch. 11

10   If I don't go through two training sessions a day, I cannot
measure up to what the public are entitled to expect.
Jonah Barrington
Sunday Times, 29 October 1989

11   Everyone can improve both their performance and enjoyment with effort, but real champions have to be prepared to suffer
and their coaches have to be ready to set them an example.
Jonah Barrington
Ibid.

12   Most people practise too little and play too much.
John Beddington
Play Better Squash, 1977, Ch. 5

13   The thing about a squash court is, there is no room for losers.
Mick Brown
Sunday Times, 1 March 1987

14   Squash is an intensely physical game.
Alan Colburn
Squash: The Ambitious Player's Guide, 1981, Pt. II

15   It's a lot of work moving thirteen stone around the court.
Don't you think I lie in bed sometimes wishing like hell I was built
like Jansher?
Chris Dittmar
Observer, 12 November 1989

16   Squash rackets is essentially a game of contrasts: brief
periods of rapid balanced movement separated by similarly brief
periods of alert stillness; hard hit strokes intermingled with shots
of the utmost delicacy.
J. T. Hankinson
Squash Racket, 1949, Ch. 1

17   The greatest area where improvement is possible is in the
mind of the player.
R. B. Hawkey
Improving Your Squash, 1967, Ch. 1

18   Fitness for squash can be best obtained by playing squash.
R. B. Hawkey
Improving Your Squash, 1972, Ch. 3

19   Your rate of improvement is certain to be geared very closely
to the number of times you actually strike a squash ball with a
squash racket against a squash court wall.
Dick Hawkey
Starting Squash, 1975, Ch. 6

20   There are three types of injury, which I always group under
the headings suicide, homicide and mutual.
Dick Hawkey
Squash Rules, Marking and Refereeing, 1980, Ch. 2

21   To walk from the squash court to the dressing room as weak
as a kitten, sweat dripping off you but mind as clear as tomorrow's
dawn, is better than five reefers or a trip on LSD.
John Hopkins
John Samuel, *The Guardian Book of Sports Quotes*, 1985

22   Cat never takes eye from bird it tries to catch and never you take eye away from ball you want to hit.

Hashim Khan with Richard E. Randall
Squash Racquets, 1967, Ch. 3

23   I went out to chase everything she [Robyn Lambourne] threw at me because, even if you don't make the return, that tends to disrupt your opponent's concentration.

Martine Le Moignan
Daily Telegraph, 11 March 1989

24   I find it [squash] boring – I play it enough, why talk about it?

Martine Le Moignan
Observer, 2 April 1989

25   It is insufficient to know that one *can* make a certain stroke; one must also know *how* and *why* one makes it.

Eustace Miles
Charles R. Read, *Squash Rackets,* 1929, Ch. 1

26   There is no harder fighter than a top junior. They are tactically brilliant because they are naturally devious.

Norman Norrington
Observer, 17 September 1989

27   Good tuition early in a squash player's career is worth pearls and diamonds.

Brian Phillips
Tackle Squash Rackets This Way, 1960, Ch. 1

28   Girls are lucky in that there are men. Men can quite easily be persuaded to take an interest in girls and squash-playing men can be very useful to squash-playing girls who wish to get on and improve their game.

Brian Phillips
Ibid., Ch. 6

29   Most explanations of the correct grip say 'shake hands with the racket'.

Edna R. Premble
Play Better Squash, 1969, Ch. 1

30   It is far better to win in a canter, or to over-handicap yourself, than to reduce your standard of play to suit that of an adversary.

Charles R. Read
Squash Rackets, 1929, Ch. I, Pt. 3

31   Even if your opponent drives the ball into one of your most tender parts, smile, accept his apology as you would accept a fat legacy, and remember that the last thing the opponent intended was to hurt you.

Charles R. Read
Ibid., Ch. V, Pt. 1

32   A painting should move. It is an idealized version of action. Body balance and movement count a lot in both [painting and squash]. In painting you have to be alert to what is happening – what is available to you by way of materials at any given moment. You have to be aware of your own thinking. Squash has that same kind of focusing of energy in the right direction. You get tuned into the action. The fun is making the ball go and mixing it up.

Frank Stella
New York Times, 30 May 1986

92   STOCK CAR RACING

See also 61 Motor Racing
62 Motor Rallying

1   I just love the excitement – especially bashing into people at speed.

Vanessa Nichols (aged fifteen)
Observer, 6 August 1989

2   All you do is go to the knacker's yard, find a shell, stick in an engine – according to category – a roll cage, do a rebore, doctor the carb and change the cam and you're in business.

Dave Smith
Observer, 6 August 1989

93 STOOLBALL

1   Stoolball . . . A play where balls are driven from stool to stool.
Samuel Johnson (1709–84)
Dictionary of the English Language, 1755

2   Stool-ball . . . consists in simply setting a stool upon the
ground, and one of the players takes his place before it, while his
antagonist, standing at a distance, tosses a ball with the intention
of striking the stool; and this it is the business of the former to
prevent by beating it away with the hand, reckoning one to the
game for every stroke of the ball; if, on the contrary, it should be
missed by the hand and touch the stool, the players change places.
Joseph Strutt (1749–1802)
The Sports and Pastimes of the People of England, 1801, Bk. II, Ch. III, XI

3   Stoolball was designed for ladies to play, and people follow it
because, as ladies play it, grace and elegance go with the game.
Stan Walker
The Times, 24 March 1989

94 SWIMMING

See also 95 Synchronized Swimming
105 Water Polo

1   All I could think about was, 'What's one-hundredth of a
second?' Maybe if I had grown my fingernails a little bit longer or
kicked a little harder, I could have won.
Matt Biondi
New York Times, 22 September 1988

2   To me, the sea is like a person – like a child that I've known a
long time. It sounds crazy, I know, but when I swim in the sea I talk
to it. I never feel alone when I'm out there.
Gertrude Ederle (in 1956 – thirty years after becoming the first woman to swim the
English Channel)
James Beasley Simpson, *Best Quotes of '54, '55, '56,* 1957

3   When I was thirteen I had this fierce feeling to go to the Olympic Games. I achieved that and now I am aiming to get there a second time, but now to win a medal.
Duncan Goodhew
The Times, 10 August 1978

4   He must needes swim that is hold up by the chinne.
John Heywood (1506–65)
Proverbs, 1546, Pt. I, Ch. V

5   No man I suppose leaps at once into deep water who does not know how to swim.
Samuel Johnson (1709–84)
Johnsonian Miscellanies, 1897, Vol. I

6   Michael Gross, the unbeatable swimmer, was beaten tonight.
Frank Litsky
New York Times, 4 August 1984

7   I can't think of anything better than breaking an American's world record in an American pool.
Adrian Moorhouse
Independent, 8 July 1989

8   They lie on a rush float, so as not to work so hard, and so to swim more easily and use their arms.
Plautus (254–184 BC)
Aulularia, Act IV

9   [At a beach near Hippo] people of all ages spend their time fishing, boating and swimming, especially the boys who have plenty of time to play. They compete in swimming out into the deep water, and the winner is the one who has left the shore and his fellow swimmers far behind.
Pliny the Younger (Gaius Plinius Caecilius Secundus, AD c. 61–c. 112)
Letters, IX, 33

10   As two spent swimmers that do cling together
And choke their art.
William Shakespeare (1564–1616)
Macbeth, 1605–6, Act I, Sc. II

11 Like an unpractis'd swimmer plunging still
    With too much labour drowns for want of skill.
William Shakespeare (1564–1616)
The Rape of Lucrece, 1593–94

12 *Trinculo:* I can swim like a duck, I'll be sworn.
    Stephano: Though thou canst swim like a duck, thou are
             made like a goose.
William Shakespeare (1564–1616)
The Tempest, 1611, Act II, Sc. II

13 The moustache helps my swimming. It catches the water and
keeps it out of my mouth.
Mark Spitz
The Times, 23 August 1972

14 This is the purest exercise of health,
    The kind refresher of the summer heats;
    Nor, when cold Winter keens the brightening flood
    Would I, weak-shivering, linger on the brink.
James Thomson (1700–48)
The Seasons: Summer, 1727

95 SYNCHRONIZED SWIMMING

1 Synchronized swimming. Call that a sport? All you see is a leg
sticking out of the water.
Eric Bristow
Independent, 14 January 1989

96 TABLE TENNIS

See also 98 Tennis

1 If millions of Americans played table tennis, we'd be good at it
too.
Insook Bhushan
New York Times, 26 September 1988

2 Most people have at some time or another tried their hand at the amiable and somewhat haphazard variety of table tennis played on the dining-room table, with any old bat, any old ball and, very often, with any old rules.

Jack Carrington
Modern Table Tennis, 1960, Ch. 1

3 Training in table tennis for young people after work and for children after school is a way to promote interest in physical fitness and body building, and to lay a good foundation for perfecting the techniques and upgrading the standard of table tennis.

Ding Shu De and others
The Chinese Book of Table Tennis, 1981, 'Teaching and Training'

4 Most of the world's top players are attackers . . . Defenders are unlikely to get to the top.

Desmond Douglas
Winning at Table Tennis, 1980, Ch. 4

5 Before a match . . . I try to think aggressively. For example, before one match we watched the Tyson-Berbick fight on video and it was great. I like to watch the brutal side of sport to put me in the right frame of mind. I want to kill the other guy. Self-controlled aggression I call it.

Desmond Douglas
Guardian, 14 February 1987

6 I feel comfortable with table tennis around me, like an old blanket.

Desmond Douglas
Ibid.

7 The trouble here [in Britain] is that table tennis is still ping pong.

Desmond Douglas
Financial Times, 3 September 1988

8 Ask the next ten people you meet if they have ever played the game. You will be amazed at how many not only say they did but still do.

English Table Tennis Association brochure.

9   Always remember, the champion is a worker as well as an artist, and the champion of the future will have to be something of a superman.
Johnny Leach
Table Tennis Complete, 1960, Ch. I

10   Always think of the bat as an extension of the playing arm.
Johnny Leach
Table Tennis in the 'Seventies, 1971, Ch. 3

11   Good players don't necessarily make good captains.
Johnny Leach
Ibid., Ch. 7

---

97 TELEVISION

See also 65 Newspapers

---

1   If TV can do what it did for golf, the most boring sport in the history of the world, imagine what it could do for us [volleyball professionals].
Leonard Armato
Independent, 30 November 1989

2   Well, that's the magic of television, isn't it? You hype the sound up a bit, point the cameras where the crowd is thickest, cut out all the boring rubbish, and you've got a Big Match.
Ted Ayling
Observer, 'Quotes of the Year', 19 December 1982

3   Television is a confounded nuisance, with gangs of scruffy men wandering about ruining the occasion.
Peter Coni
Observer, 'Quotes of the Year', 19 December 1982

4   Television has democratized the enjoyment of sport.
The Economist, 23 January 1988

5   It's the media that's changed, not Carl Lewis.
Carl Lewis
Independent, 23 July 1988

6   Television controls the game of golf. It's a matter of the tail wagging the dog.

Jack Nicklaus
Sunday Times, 3 June 1984

7   Darts is the ultimate sporting theatre as the audience is closer at the critical moment than in any other event. When the camera zooms in you can almost feel the players' dry throats.

Keith Phillips
Observer, 7 January 1990

98   TENNIS

See also 96 Table Tennis

1   I wish I had a penny for every time somebody came up and told me not to let anyone affect what I am doing for tennis.

Andre Agassi
Observer, 26 March 1989

2   Tennis ... was too gladiatorial for me, I didn't enjoy it enough.

Princess Anne
The Times, 18 October 1989

3   Anyone for tennis?

Anonymous

4   Remember that the game is won far more by the head than by the racket.

Anonymous
Norman H. Patterson, *Lawn Tennis Courtcraft*, 1934, Ch. I

5   Tennis is not a popular sport in this country [England] Wimbledon is.

Anonymous

6   I learned to play tennis because the tennis courts were the closest athletic facility to my house. But I liked tennis best anyway. I wasn't big enough then for football; I wasn't tall enough for basketball; and soccer wasn't in vogue yet.
Arthur Ashe
New York Times, 14 July 1985

7   Tennis is a game of no use in itself, but of great use in respect it maketh a quick eye and a body ready to put itself into all sorts of postures.
Francis Bacon (1561–1626)
The Advancement of Learning, 1605, Bk. II, VIII, 2

8   Tennis is such an ego sport. It creeps into everything you do.
Sue Barker
Observer, 'Sayings of the Week', 1 November 1981

9   Top tennis is overpaid.
Sue Barker
Observer, 'Sayings of the Week', 23 May 1982

10   Every point is precious. Every one we lose is a knife that cuts deep, hurts and tends to undermine our confidence.
John M. Barnaby
Racket Work: The Key to Tennis, 1969, Pt. III, Ch. 15

11   Doubles is the better half of tennis.
John M. Barnaby
Ibid., Pt. IV, Ch. 16

12   There's a lot more to life than tennis.
Carling Basset
Observer, 'Sayings of the Week', 24 June 1984

13   Girls are a distraction and can easily cost points.
Boris Becker
Observer, 'Sayings of the Week', 15 June 1986

14   It's all about self-belief and a sense of proportion. I say to myself that the worst thing I can do is lose a tennis match.
Boris Becker
Daily Telegraph, 4 November 1989

15   When I was forty, my doctor advised me that a man in his forties shouldn't play tennis. I heeded his advice carefully and could hardly wait until I reached fifty to start again.

Hugo Black
Laurence J. Peter, *Peter's Quotations*, 1977

16   Tennis anyone?

Humphrey Bogart (1899–1957)
Attributed

17   I feel that I have a little bit of an advantage when I play against him [Guillermo Villas], probably because I have beaten him so many times.

Bjorn Borg
New York Times, 12 June 1978

18   I want to be known as the best player of all time.

Bjorn Borg
New York Times, 8 July 1979

19   For sheer enjoyment, thrills and satisfaction you can't beat a good game of doubles between two evenly matched teams of the first rank. There is more fun in doubles, both for the players and the spectators.

J. Donald Budge
William F. Talbert and Bruce S. Old, *The Game of Doubles in Tennis*, 1957, Ch. 1

20   Mental fitness is just about the most envied thing in the game, because it is the hardest to achieve and consequently the most difficult to break down when opposed by it.

Angela Buxton
Tackle Lawn Tennis This Way, 1958, Ch. 4

21   It's quite clear that Virginia Wade is thriving on the pressure now that the pressure on her to do well is off.

Harry Carpenter
Private Eye, No. 563, 15 July 1983

22   You've got to go out there and play instinctively. If you think too much you get confused and you get into more trouble than it's worth. If the ball is there, hit it.

Pat Cash
Sunday Times, 5 July 1987

23   In tennis, ambition must come first and then money is a foregone conclusion. Those who put money first stay mediocre. You can't win Wimbledon by being a spoilt millionaire.

Philippe Chatrier
Observer, 1 March 1987

24   If two guys are the two best in the world, every time they go out they are at each other's nuts all the time. I'm in there fighting my butt off, and he's doing the same. There's no riding out hot streaks, and no waiting for cold streaks to end. You must stay in there, and hope, and if that's not good enough then you're finished.

Jimmy Connors
Sunday Times, 3 July 1977

25   Some days you're just one step slow.

Jimmy Connors
New York Times, 24 August 1980

26   They can give all the coaching they want. But once a guy gets down there on court, he's got to hit the ball himself.

Jimmy Connors
The Times, 5 June 1984

27   I never really knew what it meant to communicate with somebody else.

Jimmy Connors
Observer, 'Sayings of the Week', 7 June 1987

28   My game has always been to stay in until I die.

Jimmy Connors
New York Times, 26 June 1988

29   The problem is that when you get it [experience], you're too damned old to do anything about it.

Jimmy Connors
Sports Illustrated, 5 September 1988

30   You can remember me any way you want to. I don't really care, to be honest.

Jimmy Connors
Independent, 'Quotes of the Week', 1 July 1989

31   Nobody reminds me of me, I'm an original.
Jimmy Connors
Sunday Telegraph, 'Quotes 1989', 24 December 1989

32   Connors is going to have to play without making the sort of errors he didn't make in the third set.
Mark Cox
Private Eye, No. 667, 10 July 1987

33   Most people seem to think anticipation is a cross between guesswork and a gift from heaven ... Now there are many essentials that a first-class lawn tennis player must have, but clairvoyance is not one of them.
Evelyn Dewhurst
Lawn Tennis Guaranteed, 1939, Ch. XII

34   It's usually not up to the other girl. I either win matches or lose them.
Jo Durie
Sunday Times, 5 June 1983

35   It's hard to find the balance between winning and trying to improve.
Jo Durie
The Times, 20 June 1984

36   When I have played a good first set I panic and start worrying about how I won it.
Jo Durie
Guardian, 5 October 1989

37   If I'm the No. 1 in Britain, things must be pretty bad. . . . At the moment we are down and out and it's going to take a long time to get back up again. There are not enough kids playing the game, too many people asking what's wrong and not enough getting on with putting it right.
Jo Durie
The Times, 26 October 1989

38   That's my whole game, playing steady and letting them make errors. I win more games that way than by hitting winners.
Chris Evert
The Times, 1 August 1972

39   I was going to choose football, but there are eleven in a team and if you lose you can blame everyone else. In tennis, you can't.
Philip Gainford
The Times, 8 April 1989

40   The tennis match isn't over . . . well, until it's over.
Robert Gensemer
Tennis, 1969, Ch. 1

41   Men's tennis and women's tennis are different sports. We're rock and roll; they're classical.
Vitas Gerulaitis
Sydney Morning Herald, 'Sayings of the Week', 3 August 1985

42   If my opponents don't beat me, I'll probably beat myself.
Steffi Graf
Guardian, 20 January 1990

43   It is true to say that Wimbledon tickets are now safer than the currencies of many countries.
Buzzer Hadingham
Independent, 'Quotes of the Week', 14 January 1989

44   Suppose one does become an expert tennis player, then what?
Frank McKinney Hubbard (1868–1930)
New Sayings by Abe Martin, 1917

45   It's better that they still treat me as a sixteen-year-old. I think I'd rather be a kid playing tennis and enjoying it.
Andrea Jaeger
Sunday Times, 21 June 1981

46   I wanted to be patient and wait for her [Chris Evert Lloyd] to make a mistake. I really didn't want to go to the net or do something else that was stupid.
Andrea Jaeger (who won, in 1982)
Jack L. Groppel, *Tennis for Advanced Players,* 1984, Ch. 7

47   [Tennis] is an individual sport. You have to be selfish.
Andrea Jaeger
Observer, 1 September 1985

48   Steffi Graf has now won forty-two consecutive matches, winning all of them.
Christine Janes, BBC Radio 2
Private Eye, No. 706, 6 January 1989

49   Wimbledon championships are won on the practice court.
C. M. Jones and Angela Buxton
Starting Lawn Tennis, 1975, Ch. 6

50   We've got to get women's tennis off the women's pages and into the sports pages.
Billie Jean King
Barbara Rowes, *The Book of Quotes*, 1979

51   When you stop having fun, you don't win.
Billie Jean King
New York Times, 24 June 1979

52   You only play as well as you have to.
Billie Jean King
New York Times, 17 March 1980

53   My idea of keeping fit for tennis . . . is to play tennis.
Rod Laver
Doug Ibbotson, *Sporting Scenes*, 1980, Ch. 9

54   My concentration is intense the whole day before a match. If things around me are unusual . . . I cannot get them out of my mind on the court. On tour, I want things exactly as they have been ten thousand times before.
Ivan Lendl
Sunday Times, 21 March 1982

55   I'll buy John McEnroe his ticket and hotel next year, so everyone can pick on him instead.
Ivan Lendl
The Times, 1 January 1987

56   It is not good for me to let excitement take over my mind. I'm the player who has to think before each point.
Ivan Lendl
Sunday Times, 5 July 1987

57   I don't like playing under lights. Evenings are for dinner or watching hockey.
Ivan Lendl
Daily Telegraph, 11 March 1989

58   You have to win; you don't have to play perfect. I would rather win any time than play perfect and lose.
Ivan Lendl
Guardian, 27 January 1990

59   A tennis-ball, whether in motion by the stroke of a racket, or lying still at rest, is not by anyone taken to be a free agent. If we enquire into the reason, we shall find it is, because we conceive not a tennis-ball to think, and consequently not to have any volition.
John Locke (1632–1704)
An Essay Concerning Human Understanding, 1690, Bk. II, Ch. XXI, 9

60   I am not saying women umpires are no good. It's just harder to get upset with a lady in the chair.
John McEnroe
Observer, 'Sayings of the Week', 21 June 1981

61   I've never tolerated phoneyness in anyone and there's a lot of phoneyness at Wimbledon.
John McEnroe
Observer, 'Sayings of the Week', 16 August 1981

62   I've never been fined for saying something obscene. It's always been for saying something like 'You're the pits' or something.
John McEnroe
Observer, 'Sayings of the Week', 22 November 1981

63   I was only talking to myself.
John McEnroe
Observer, 'Sayings of the Year', 3 January 1982

64   I don't think I've got all the enjoyment I should have got out of tennis.
John McEnroe
Sunday Times, 13 June 1982

65   I wasn't happy when the umpire told the spectators to be quiet. That only encourages them to make more noise.

John McEnroe
Observer, 'Sayings of the Week', 27 June 1982

66   Tennis players are very sensitive people.

John McEnroe
Observer, 'Sayings of the Week', 26 June 1983

67   In years to come I'll be thanked for what I've done for tennis.

John McEnroe
Sunday Times, 24 June 1984

68   One of me is worth forty thousand of you.

John McEnroe (to the crowd at the Queen's Club tournament)
Ibid.

69   Being a celebrity is like being raped. You can't do anything about it.

John McEnroe
Sydney Morning Herald, 'Sayings of the Week', 30 November 1985

70   You're sore from playing when you're in a tournament . . . then you have a couple of weeks off and you're sore for *not* playing while you're resting.

John McEnroe
Sunday Times, 4 May 1986

71   I think tennis has missed me – I don't think there is much question about that.

John McEnroe
Observer, 'Sayings of the Week', 10 August 1986

72   If I get out of bed and find I can't walk, I won't play.

John McEnroe (following a hip injury)
Observer, 22 March 1987

73   I didn't realize what things were about until I took time off. I needed time to re-evaluate my life, to find out who I am, where I want to go. What is important for me is to enjoy the sport. I put too much pressure on myself before.

John McEnroe
Independent, 12 November 1988

74   When you play tennis out there you're really exposing your whole soul.
John McEnroe
Independent, 'Quotes of the Week', 15 July 1989

75   We all make too much money, period. We're perceived as selfish, but then so are a lot of athletes.
John McEnroe
Sunday Times, 10 September 1989

76   We'll all be turning into money whores if we can't turn our backs on certain things and I hope I'm not known as that when people look back on my career.
John McEnroe
Guardian, 28 October 1989

77   Hopefully people will remember the way I played the game more than the way I acted at times.
John McEnroe
Sunday Times, 11 February 1990

78   Every match is a different puzzle.
Tim Mayotte
Sunday Times, 26 June 1983

79   I was brought up to respect people but, on a tennis court, this can be dangerous.
Tim Mayotte
Ibid.

80   Temper is not a match-winning attribute.
Paul Metzler
Advanced Tennis, 1967, Ch. 1

81   If you see a tennis player who looks as if he is working very hard, then that means he isn't very good.
Helen Wills Moody
Laurence J. Peter, *Peter's Quotations*, 1977

82   The more I see of tennis, the more I'm convinced that grass is not a good surface to play on unless it is hard and in perfect condition: as, for example, at Wimbledon. It is easy on the eye and the feet. But that is all that can be said for it.
Tony Mottram
The Times, 16 August 1972

83   It's like a second Christmas every time I come to Wimbledon.
Ilie Nastase
New York Times, 26 June 1983

84   Getting angry helps for people like us. It makes you fight hard. Everything becomes a war.
Ilie Nastase
Independent, 'Quotes of the Week', 8 July 1989

85   Wimbledon is so special, it's overwhelming. Even on the side courts when you're nobody, and then when you're on the centre court in the final, there's nothing else like it.
Martina Navratilova
New York Times, 16 July 1978

86   Do you know the difference between involvement and commitment? Think of ham and eggs. The chicken is involved. The pig is committed.
Martina Navratilova
Observer, 'Sayings of the Week', 5 September 1982

87   It's OK when you roll someone over, but it's so much more exciting and satisfying when [a match] is close.
Martina Navratilova
Tennis Great Britain 1985

88   I don't like anyone to beat me twice in a row.
Martina Navratilova
Sunday Times, 19 June 1988

89   Half an inch and it's a great serve. Half an inch can change your career.
Martina Navratilova
Observer, 17 September 1989

90   If you give spectators a good time, they'll give it back . . .
We're not clowns, we want to win. But if there's a situation where
we can have fun, all the better.
Yannick Noah
Sunday Telegraph, 19 March 1989

91   Walking through White Hall, I heard the King was gone to
play at Tennis, so I down to the New Tennis Court, and saw him
and Sir Arthur Slingsby play against my Lord of Suffolke and my
Lord Chesterfield. The King beat three, and lost two sets, they all,
and he particularly, playing well, I thought.
Samuel Pepys (1633–1703)
Diary, 28 December 1663

92   To the Tennis Court . . . and there saw the King play at
tennis and others: but to see how the King's play was extolled,
without any cause at all, was a loathsome sight though sometimes,
indeed, he did play very well, and deserved to be commended; but
such open flattery is beastly.
Samuel Pepys (1633–1703)
Ibid., 4 January 1663–4

93   The King, playing at tennis, had a steele-yard carried to him;
and I was told it was to weigh him after he had done playing; and at
noon Mr Ashburnham told me that it is only the King's curiosity,
which he usually hath of weighing himself before and after his
play, to see how much he loses in weight by playing: and this day
he lost 4½ lbs.
Samuel Pepys (1633–1703)
Ibid., 2 September 1667

94   The four-handed game [doubles], well played, is the art of
lawn tennis at its highest.
Fred Perry
William F. Talbert and Bruce S. Old, *The Game of Doubles in Tennis,* 1957, Ch. 1

95   If you're fit you play. If you're not, you don't. No alibis.
Fred Perry
Attributed

96   One man in a thousand can play tennis through his fifties – witness William Randolph Hearst. But the rest of us must drop it early or it will drop us with a bang.
Walter B. Pitkin (1878–1953)
Tryon Edwards, *The New Dictionary of Thoughts*

97   Nothing is more spectacular than a first-class doubles match; even more than singles play, the doubles game provides a test of generalship and resourcefulness that challenges the utmost concentration and ingenuity of the player.
Vincent Richards
William F. Talbert and Bruce S. Old, *The Game of Doubles in Tennis*, 1957, Ch. 1

98   Billie Jean King, with the look on her face that says she can't believe it . . . because she never believes it, and yet, somehow, I think she does.
Max Robertson
Private Eye, No. 539, 13 August 1982

99   These ball boys are marvellous. You don't even notice them. There's a left-handed one over there. I noticed him earlier.
Max Robertson
Private Eye, No. 563, 15 July 1983

100   McEnroe is the last player to win with beauty instead of brute force.
Manuel Santana
Independent, 'Quotes of the Week', 15 July 1989

101   The key to my game is to serve and volley. You can't cover all the court.
Pam Shriver
New York Times, 17 August 1980

102   The qualifications of a fine gentleman are to eat *à la mode*, drink champagne, dance jigs, and play at tennis.
Thomas Shadwell (c. 1642–92)
The Sullen Lovers, 1668, Act II

103   Falling out at tennis.
William Shakespeare (1564–1616)
Hamlet, 1599–1600, Act II, Sc. I

104   *King Henry:*   What treasure, uncle?

      Duke of Exeter: Tennis-balls, my liege.

      King Henry: We are glad the dauphin is so pleasant
          with us;
      His present and your pains we thank you
          for;
      When we have match'd our rackets to
          these balls,
      We will, in France, by God's grace, play
          a set
      Shall strike his father's crown into the
          hazard.
      Tell him he hath made a match with
          such a wrangler
      That all the courts of France will be
          disturb'd
      With chases.

William Shakespeare (1564–1616)
Henry V, 1598–99, Act I, Sc. II

105   The faith they have in tennis.
William Shakespeare (1564–1616)
Henry VIII, 1612–13, Act I, Sc. III

    106   A man, whom both the waters and the wind
        In that vast tennis-court hath made the ball
        For them to play upon.
        William Shakespeare (1564–1616)
        Pericles, 1608–9, Act II, Sc. I

107   When I play tennis I can take out my anger by slamming the
ball harder, but in golf you can't afford to get mad or excited.
Jan Stephenson
New York Times, 8 May 1978

108   Players watch the ball whereas a line-judge watches the line.
A stationary line-judge has a better chance of making an accurate
call.
Herbert Syndercombe
The Times, 26 July 1984

109   Doubles is not just singles with two players on each side of the net instead of one.
William F. Talbert and Bruce S. Old
The Game of Doubles in Tennis, 1957, Ch. 1

110   Singles is a game of imagination, doubles is a game of exact angles.
Bill Tilden
William F. Talbert and Bruce S. Old, *The Game of Doubles in Tennis*, 1957, Ch. 1

111   I had to take two extra valium because I thought the dress was going to lose.
Ted Tinling (having designed a lucky dress for Martina Navratilova)
New York Times, 9 July 1978

112   Tennis is eighty per cent head and twenty per cent legs.
Ion Tiriac
Sydney Morning Herald, 'Sayings of 1985', 28 December 1985

113   Dis game of tennis, she drop dead if McEnroe don't come back soon.
Ion Tiriac
The Times, 1 January 1987

114   I wanted to be a complete person. It was a cop out in a way. If you commit yourself to be the number one in tennis you have to be totally blinkered and cut off a whole part of yourself.
Virginia Wade
Sunday Times, 12 July 1981

115   Tennis is a fine balance between determination and tiredness.
Virginia Wade
Jonathon Green, *A Dictionary of Contemporary Quotations*, 1982

116   I am playing for fun. But it's more fun if you win.
Virginia Wade
New York Times, 26 June 1983

117   An old player being recycled for the good of the sport.
Virginia Wade
Observer, 'Sayings of the Week', 28 April 1985

118   One should go on court and assert oneself.
Virginia Wade
The Times, 28 September 1985

119   To make it in the big world of tennis it is not enough to be
'good enough', 'technically good' or even simply 'talented'. You
have to be technically perfect to compete and live with the
machines churned out by foreign schools.
Virginia Wade
Independent, 23 March 1989

120   Steffi [Graf] has a tremendous presence when you're
standing right next to her.
Virginia Wade, BBC1
Private Eye, No. 720, 21 July 1989

121   We are merely the stars' tennis-balls, struck and bandied
which way please them.
John Webster (c. 1580–c. 1625)
The Duchess of Malfi, 1623, Act IV

122   I rank only number five in the world. You aren't going to sell
any more papers by talking with me.
Mats Wilander
Sunday Times, 1 May 1983

123   For sure, Borg was my god . . . But I'm Mats not Bjorn.
Mats Wilander
Ibid.

124   I think I have to improve my service . . . and I guess my
volley, and my forehand and my backhand and then my footwork
[to win Wimbledon].
Mats Wilander
Sunday Telegraph, 'Quotes 1989', 24 December 1989

125   For the first time a record Wimbledon attendance.
Gerald Williams
Private Eye, No. 642, 25 July 1986

126   [Doubles is] . . . a game entirely by itself.
Helen Wills
William F. Talbert and Bruce S. Old, *The Game of Doubles in Tennis,* 1957, Ch. 1

99   TRIATHLON

1   Swimming is great for non-stress build-up. Cycling is good for a cardiovascular workout without killing yourself. For me, the tough part of the triathlon is the running.
Alison Roe
New York Times, 30 May 1986

100   TRIPLE JUMP

1   There's no other event like it [the triple jump]. Those three bounces are a thing of beauty. The art form of the event and raising the consciousness of the spectators comes first; winning comes second.
Ron Livers
New York Times, 5 June 1978

101   TROPHIES

1   Most of my trophies get put in the loft but what makes this one special is that you can't win it [his MBE].
Eric Bristow
Independent, 'Quotes of the Week', 7 January 1989

102   TUG-OF-WAR

1   Any man of surly disposition given to frequent grousing is much better left out.
Anonymous
Tug-of-war coaching guidelines

2   In 1952, when I was an apprentice, the chap opposite me was involved [in tug-of-war]. I bet him I could beat him and he won. I went away, got fit, and three weeks later I challenged him to double or quits and won. I was hooked.

Peter Craft
Independent, 15 October 1988

3   When Greeks joyn'd Greeks, then was the tug of war!

Nathaniel Lee (1653?–92)
The Rival Queens, 1677, Act IV, Sc. II

103   VOLLEYBALL

1   Good volleyball rests on fluent court movement.

Don Anthony
Success in Volleyball, 2nd ed., 1978, 'Conditioning'

2   Volleyball has all the elements you could want: fast action, guys diving, guys with no shirts, the sun, the beach and girls in bikinis.

Leonard Armato
Independent, 30 November 1989

3   We decided to fund the men rather than the women because there's more strength in depth at the present time.

Richard Callicott, Chairman of the English Volleyball Association (on the funding for a national men's squad)
Independent, 29 July 1989

4   You get people who think volleyball is something you play at picnics, or that it's a sport for girls.

Bob Ctvrtlik
New York Times, 15 July 1988

5   Volleyball is still in its salad days of innocence in this country – it has that tell-tale mix of evangelizing zeal and pleasing pay-to-play amateurishness.

Chris Curtain
Guardian, 16 March 1987

6   Just as individual notes make up a symphony, the individual skills of volleyball make up the game; and just as one false note in a piece of music mars the whole composition, one action inefficiently carried out in volleyball can ruin the whole match.

Barrie MacGregor
Volleyball, 1977, 'Skills'

7   If you leave a net up overnight it's gone next morning. In fact, we have to keep an eye on the net while we're playing [at Sheep Meadow, New York].

Marty Shapiro
New York Times, 31 July 1978

104   WALKING

1   'Will you walk a little faster?' said a whiting to a snail,
     'There's a porpoise close behind, us, and he's treading on my
        tail.'

Lewis Carroll (1832–98)
Alice's Adventures in Wonderland, 1865, Ch. 10

2   I nauseate walking; 'tis a country diversion; I loathe the country.

William Congreve (1670–1729)
The Way of the World, 1700, Act III, Sc. XII

3   I love to lose myself in other men's minds. When I am not walking, I am reading; I cannot sit and think. Books think for me.

Charles Lamb (1775–1834)
Last Essays of Elia, 1833, 'Detached Thoughts on Books and Reading'

4   Who fastest walks, but walks astray,
     Is only furthest from his way.

   Matthew Prior (1664–1721)
   Alma, 1718, Canto III

105 WATER POLO

1   When you get to the Olympic level you expect perfection.
Perfection is to block every shot.

Craig Wilson
New York Times, 2 August 1984

106 WATER SKIING

1   The problem with water skiing is the risk of a thirty-mile-an-
hour enema.

Anonymous

107 WEIGHT LIFTING

1   Canadian Weightlifters: Three clean and four jerks.

Anonymous (graffiti after four Canadian lifters had been caught drug-taking)
Independent, 'Quotes of the Olympic Games', 1 October 1988

2   Weight lifting is something you really have to love.

John Bergman
New York Times, 23 September 1988

3   In many ways the sport is more feminine than masculine.
Women are more supple and have a lower centre of gravity, which
are two of the things that you need for weightlifting.

Sally Jones
The Times, 24 November 1986

4   You have to be one hundred per cent positive in your thinking. If you go up on to the platform with any doubt at all in your mind about lifting the weights, you probably won't make it.
Terry Manton
New York Times, 13 May 1979

5   The mental approach [to weight lifting] is vital.
Pat Omori
New York Times, 13 May 1979

108   WIND SURFING

1   Wind surfers do it standing up.
Anonymous

2   Windsurfing . . . looks like a very physical sport, but it isn't at all. You just lean back, like water-skiing.
Steve Cowan
New York Times, 12 June 1978

109   WINNING AND LOSING

1   Winning can be defined as the science of being totally prepared.
George Allen
Attributed

2   If a sportsman gets to the top there is only one way left to go.
Anonymous

3   Win as if you were used to it, lose as if you liked it.
Anonymous

4   I always said I might cry if I won but never if I lost.
Lillian Board
The Times, 17 October 1968

5   One gold is better than two silvers.
Mary Decker
Observer, 'Sayings of the Week', 29 July 1984

6   I can't see any reason why you can't be a champion and a nice human being.
Jo Durie
Sunday Times, 5 June 1983

7   The business of winning medals and doing well in international sport is the icing on the cake, but not the fruit of sport.
Duke of Edinburgh
Observer, 'Sayings of the Week', 26 June 1988

8   Players win games and players lose games—it's all about players really.
Bobby Ferguson
Private Eye, No. 554, 11 March 1983

9   You don't mind suffering for a gold medal. You expect it.
Brendan Foster
The Times, 8 August 1978

10   In all games, it is good to leave off a winner.
Thomas Fuller (1654–1734)
Gnomologia, 1732, No. 2812

11   It is a silly game, where no body wins.
Thomas Fuller (1654–1734)
Ibid., No. 2880

12   He laugth that winth.
John Heywood (1506–65)
Proverbs, 1546, Pt. I, Ch. V

13   He who wishes to achieve the longed for victory in a race, must have trained long and hard as a boy, have sweated and groaned, and abstained from wine and women.
Horace (Quintus Horatius Flaccus 65–8 BC)
Ars Poetica, 412

14   The cheerful loser is the winner.
Frank McKinney Hubbard (1868–1930)
Epigrams, 1923

15   Winners are people who do their best. They don't necessarily win gold medals. I've seen people win medals who were never winners and people who were winners who never won medals.

Dick Jochums
New York Times, 31 March 1980

16   Winning is a habit; losing is a habit. Right now our habit is winning.

Jimmy Johnson
Sports Illustrated, 12 September 1988

17   I'd rather be a poor winner than any kind of loser.

George S. Kaufman
C. Bingham, *Wit and Wisdom*, 1982

18   Motivation is more important than anything else, provided you're healthy. Winning matches depends on how much you care.

Billie Jean King
New York Times, 24 June 1979

19   The public likes to see winners lose.

Billie Jean King
New York Times, 17 March 1980

20   Winning isn't everything, it's the only thing.

Vince Lombardi
Alan Colburn, *Squash: The Ambitious Player's Guide*, 1981, Ch. 16

21   If you can conceive and believe, you will achieve.

Ed Lukowich
The Skol Book of Curling, 1982, Sec. 3

22   It's a Renaissance – or, put more simply, some you win, some you lose.

Desmond Lynam
Private Eye, No. 571, 4 November 1983

23   Losing still hurts, but that's good. When it stops hurting, that's when I stop playing.

Martina Navratilova
Independent, 'Quotes of the Week', 28 January 1989

24   [In reply to the question of whether losing was a disaster.] It is, when it's a lovely spring afternoon and you don't have anything else planned.
Jack Nicklaus
New York Times, 23 July 1978

25   Winning isn't the end of the world.
David Pleat
Private Eye, No. 664, 29 May 1987

26   Winning or not winning a world championship is not so important. It is only a transient moment in life.
Ayrton Senna
Sunday Times, 24 September 1989

27   You've got to believe that you're going to win and I believe that we'll win the World Cup until the final whistle blows and we're knocked out.
Peter Shilton
Private Eye, No. 635, 18 April 1986

28   In Britain there's a will to win; in America there's a need to win.
Glynn Tiernan
New York Times, 13 September 1988

29   Winners aren't popular. Losers often are.
Virginia Wade
Jonathon Green, *A Dictionary of Contemporary Quotations*, 1982

30   I hate to lose in anything, even checkers, chess or snooker, I hate to ease up in any game. Easing up breeds quitting.
Tom Watson
Sunday Times, 10 July 1977

110 WRESTLING

1   The two champions set forthe stripped into their dublets and
hosen, and untrussed, that they may so the better command the
use of their lymmes; and first shaking hands, in token of
friendship, they fall presently to the effect of anger; for each
striveth how to take holde of the other with his beste advantage,
and to beare his adverse party downe; wherein whosoever
overthroweth his mate, in such sort as that either his backe, or the
one shoulder and contrary heele do touch the grounde, is
accounted to give the fall. If he be only endangered and make a
narrow escape, it is called a foyle.

Richard Carew (1555–1620)
Survey of Cornwall, 1602

2   I am afraid . . . if he wrestles with me, of being torn by his sharp
nails.

Horace (Quintus Horatius Flaccus 65–8 BC)
Epistles, I, xix, 46

3   The wrestler on the sand is stronger than the one whose arms
are worn out by a long wait.

Ovid (43 BC–AD 17)
Tristia, IV, vi, 31

4   Went to Moorefields, and there walked, and stood and saw the
wrestling, which I never saw so much of before, between the north
and west countrymen.

Samuel Pepys (1633–1703)
Diary, 28 June 1661

INDEX OF KEY WORDS

This index is arranged alphabetically, both for the key words and for the entries following each key word. If the key word sought is the same as a topic title (shown in bold print), the topic title should be consulted first as this index does not usually repeat words appearing under the same topic.

For entries other than topic titles, the reference consists of two numbers, the first of which indicates the topic and the second the quotation itself. For example, the first entry is 'abstained: a. from wine and women 109.13'. This refers to the 13th quotation appearing under the 109th topic, which is 'Winning and Losing'. The numbers and titles of the topics appear at the top of the pages.

Rowing: Topic 78
Royals: A lot of the R. watch darts
    24.2
rub: r. of the green 11.2
rubs: world is full of r. 11.23
Rugby: Topic 79
    r. football was a hooligan's game
    36.65
    R. is a beastly game 35.2
rules: play by their r. 40.89
run: All you r. you win 11.12
    He can r. but he can't hide 12.67
    scoring that hundredth r. 20.96
Running: Topic 80
    call it r. because I do it for pleasure
    53.2
    Olympic event for r. backwards
    20.17
    R. a marathon 58.7
    r. barefoot across the bosoms of
    maidens 58.3
    smaller guys just look as if they're
    r. faster 7.20
runs: funny how r. breeds r. 20.12

S: five Ss – strength, speed, stamina,
    suppleness and skill 4.2
sacked: Getting s. is just part of the
    football scene 36.3
Sailing: Topic 81
salmon-fishers: now the s. moist 13.3
salmon: S. fishing is made up largely
    of beliefs 33.7
schoolboys: s. went on with their
    game of baseball 7.32
science: Boxing is a s. 12.8
    noble s. of boxing 12.46
scientists: team-doctors, s., coaches
    and so on 3.9
scoring: s. like Jane 40.100
Scot: Soccer is life itself for a S. 36.72
Scotland: What would S. be like
    without football? 36.52
Scudamore: Peter S. is in one race
    73.11
sea: finny subject of the s. 33.61
    That great fishpond, the s. 33.15
second: to be s. is even worse 83.1
secrets: no s. in basketball 8.13
selectors: s.' role should be to select
    20.48

self-confidence: biggest thing . . . is
    to have s. 66.6
self-defence: manly art of s. among
    the clergy 12.53
sex: Catching a ball is a little like s.
    for me 7.28
    Kite flying is as exciting as s. 56.1
    Like s., the movements in football
    are limited 36.1
    Rugby . . . no place for the delicate
    s. 79.23
    when it's a question of cricket or s.
    20.82
sexual intercourse: Of course a player
    can have s. 36.101
sexy: a s. woman was one who 4.1
sharp: billiard s. whom anyone
    catches 9.2
shins: players kick each other's s.
    36.104
Shooting: Topic 82
shot putters: S. must have the five Ss.
    4.2
shot: Any s. is a good s. 8.19
show business: That's s. 36.63
Showjumping: Topic 83
shuttlecock: Battledore and s. 5.5
    S., s. tell me true 5.1
    Take one s. 5.4
silvers: gold is better than two s.
    109.5
simple: Basketball is a s. game 8.8
Skateboarding: Topic 84
Skating: Topic 85
    Dressage is the nearest thing to s.
    30.3
ski: skateboard . . . water s. for dry
    land 84.1
Skiing: Topic 86
skill: Fencing . . . sport of s. 32.4
    five Ss – strength, speed, stamina,
    suppleness and s. 4.2
    most difficult s. in sport 7.15
    s. will always beat might 12.76
skirts: because of my short s. 64.1
Skittles: Topic 87
sleep: All tours . . . train, s., play and
    eat 90.36
    prize my s. 30.2
slow: strong men are s. men 52.2
Snooker: Topic 88
snoring: and he's lying there s. 12.98

INDEX OF AUTHORS AND SOURCES

In this index the entries refer to individual quotations rather than pages. Each entry contains two numbers, the first of which indicates the number of the topic and the second the actual quotation. For example, under Addison, the reference is 42.1. This refers to the 1st quotation appearing under the 42nd topic, which is 'Gymnastics'. The numbers and titles of the topics appear at the top of the pages.

Index of Authors and Sources

Index of Authors and Sources

Tugwell, Maurice, 86.16
Turberville, George, 38.11
Twain, Mark, 40.122, 90.39
Tyson, Mike, 12.93, 12.94, 12.95, 12.96, 12.97, 12.98, 12.99

Ueberroth, Peter, 7.68
Underwood, Derek, 20.102, 20.103

van Dyke, Henry, 33.69
Vardon, Harry, 40.123
Vecsey, George, 80.38
Veeck, Bill, 7.69, 7.70
Venables, Terry, 36.111, 36.112
Victoria, Queen, 57.2
Vine, David, 88.25
Virgo, John, 88.26

Waddell, Sid, 24.5
Wade, Allen, 36.113
Wade, Virginia, 98.114, 98.115, 98.116, 98.117, 98.118, 98.119, 98.120, 109.29
Wadekar, Ajit, 20.104
Wakelam, H. B. T., 78.49, 78.50
Wakiihuri, Douglas, 58.10, 58.11
Walker, Billy, 12.100
Walker, Murray, 61.27, 61.28, 61.29, 61.30
Walker, Stan, 93.3
Walsh, William, 49.34
Walton, Bill, 8.26
Walton, Izaak, 33.70, 33.71, 33.72, 33.73, 33.74, 33.75, 33.76, 33.77, 33.78, 33.79, 33.80, 33.81, 33.82, 33.83, 33.84, 33.85, 33.86, 33.87
Warbuton Lee, Philip, 49.35
Warren, William E., 8.23
Watkins, E., 36.114
Watson, John, 61.31, 61.32
Watson, Tom, 109.30
Wattana, Jimmy, 88.27
Waugh, Auberon, 12.101, 33.88
Way, Paul, 40.124
Webber, Jack, 83.4
Webster, John, 98.121
Welch, Julie, 78.51
Welch, Racquel, 35.115

Wellings, E. M., 20.105
Wells, Allan, 80.39
Wells, H. G., 33.89
Welsh, Robin, 22.6, 22.7, 22.8
West, Peter, 80.40
Wheatcroft, Geoffrey, 19.5, 38.12, 41.8
Whetton, Joe, 8.27
Wigoder, Lord, 20.106
Wilander, Mats, 98.122, 98.123, 98.124
Wilcockson, J., 23.6, 23.7
Wilde, Oscar, 31.5, 38.13, 90.40
Wilkins, Mac, 26.3
Wilkins, Ray, 36.116
Wilkinson, Gary, 88.28
Wilkinson, Howard, 36.117, 36.118
Williams, Barrie, 36.119
Williams, Gerald, 98.125
Williams, Reggie, 35.25
Williams, Rex, 88.29
Williams, Ted, 7.71
Willis, Bob, 20.107, 20.108
Wills, Helen, 98.126
Wilson, Cliff, 88.30
Wilson, Craig, 105.1
Wilson, Earl, 7.72
Wilson, Harold, 36.120
Wilson, Jocky, 24.6, 24.7
Wilson, John (Christopher North), 9.10
Wilt, Fred, 80.41
Winchell, Cheryl, 23.12
Wohlford, Jim, 7.73
Wood, Dudley, 78.52
Wood, Graeme, 20.109
Wooden, John R., 8.28, 8.29
Woodleigh, Ben, 56.2
Woosnam, Ian, 40.125, 40.126, 40.127
Wordsworth, William, 85.15
Wyche, Sam, 17.4, 35.26
Wynne, Sir Watkin, 36.121

Zatopek, Emil, 3.9
Zoeller, Fuzzy, 40.128, 40.129, 40.130
Zurbriggen, Pirmin, 86.17